Second Nature:
Earth Is Peace

Edited by
Mbizo Chirasha
and
David Swanson

Charlottesville, Va., U.S.
First edition—2020

©2020 World BEYOND War

All rights reserved. No part of this book may be reproduced or transmitted in any form or by any means, including mechanical, electric, photocopying, recording, or otherwise, without the prior written permission of the publisher.

Cover art and design by Alex McAdams

Interior design by David Swanson

Printed in the USA

First Edition / October 2020

ISBN: 978-1-7347837-3-5

Table of Contents

Introduction by David Swanson	10
Foreword by Mbizo Chirasha	11
Poems by Ngam Emmanuel	
Ty Wasteland	12
The Wars of Assimilation	13
Ascension Thursday	15
When the Election Approaches	16
Poems by Jambiya Kai	
Pokerman	18
The Secret Society	20
"What a Pretty Boy" – The Story of Juneck Livi	22
Poems by Sydney Saize	
Dry Cry	26
A Dilema	27
Shame	28
The Liberty They Were Denied	29
Ghetto Bulletins	30
Dry Season	31
The Syntactics of a Regime	32
Poems by Wilson Waison Tinotenda	
Voices from the Ashes	34
Fear	36
Poems by Aleck T Mabenge	
Burnt	38
Poems by Tshepo Phokoje	
Fear	40
Poems by Alan Britt	
Africa	42

Poems by Richmore Tera
    Child of the Struggle — 44
    Desideratum — 44
    Samosa Town — 45

Poems by Vanessa KaluKWETE
    70 Years Younger — 47
    Backyard — 48

Poems by Chrispah Munyoro
    Vultures in Disguise — 50
    Blasting of Explosives — 52
    Black Opal — 53
    Delis Uproar — 55

Poems by Geraldine Sinyuy
    Elegy for My Brother — 57

Poems by Chad Norman
    The Flagless Flagpole — 59
    Where the Path Is Melting — 61

Poems by James Coburn
    Damnation — 64
    Crossing the Bridge — 65
    Lending a Hand — 66

Poems by Sadiqullah Khan
    May I Ask — 68
    Thus Plunged Deeper — 69
    Oppressive Society — 70
    An Inauguration — 71

Poems by TemitopeAina
    Scarred — 73
    Whispers to the Broken Heart — 74

Poems by Jabulani Mzinyathi
    Honourable — 76

Poems by Nungari Kabutu Wilfred
    Black and Free   78
    Bold Face to Freedom   79

Poems by Khadijah Finesse
    No Mercy   81

Poems by Bina Sarkar Ellias
    Syrian Nightmares in Kansas City   84

Poems by Mohammed C. Jalloh
    When I Was a Slave   86
    Lost Syria   88

Poems by Nancy Ndeke
    Fired   90
    I Speak   92
    Billed But Still Barred   94

Poems by Milimo Chinimbwa
    Rhythm of Distress   96
    Cracked Calabash   97

Poems by Daniel Amakor
    Beauty Behind Scars   98
    Constructive Criticism   99

Poems by Tracey C Nicholson
    What Lies Beneath   101

Poems by Anu Soneye
    Rhythms of War   103
    How Can We Breathe?   104

Poems by Annette Swann
    Burnt Face — Forgiven   106

Poems by Caroline Adwar
    Life Changes   108

Poems by Paul Oladipo Kehinde
    Express Myself   111
    Fly With Me   112

Poems by Nwuguru Chidiebere Sullivan
    Celebration of Indignation   114
Poems by Ibrahim Clouds
    Africa — One of a Kind   117
    Is Halloween in Bangladesh   118
Poems by Opeyemi Joe
    The Oligarchs   120
Poems by Tracy Yvonne Breazile
    Osmithila   122
    Zimbabwean Voices   123
Poems by Awadifo Olga Kili
    Tanga   126
Poems by Omwa Ombara
    A Dirge of Hope to Sudan   128
    In Honor of Press Freedom Day 2020   131
Poems by Samuella J. Conteh
    Beautiful Scars   133
    Hours in Reverse   134
Poems by Michael (Dickel) Dekel
    Nothing Remembers   136
Poems by Jerusha Kananu Marete
    Smile Again Katrina   138
    Mau Mau Veteran's Wail   142
Poems by Lingiwe Patience Gumbo
    Still Here   145
    To My Unborn Child Lingiwe   147
Poems by Beatrice Othieno-Ahere
    From Chaos to New Order   151
Poems by Jamie Dedes
    One Lifetime After Another   153
Poems by Francis Otole
    Biceps and triceps   155

Poems by Rokiah Hashim
    I Am Sorry, Mir Rahman   157

Poems by Mourad Faska
    What Is Life?   160
    I Am a Wretched in the Earth of Riches   161
    Flutter and Fly Away   162
    Human beasts   163

Poems by Smeetha Bhoumik
    Making Fists and Opening Them Skyward   165

Poems by Melissa Begley
    Joyful Night   168

Poems by Nsah Mala
    Prophecies from Reptiles   170

Poems by Gorata Mighty Ntshwabi
    A Dark Cloud Hovers Over Sudan   172

Poems by Ambily Omanakuttan
    My Syria   175

Poems by Michael Mwangi Macharia
    It's Midnight in Yaounde   177
    The Common Man   178
    City Rain   178
    Nightwarriors   179

Poems by Victor WeSonga
    Recluse Poise   181

Poems by Munia Khan
    A Leaders Path   184

Poems by Kabedoopong Piddo Ddibe'st
    The Black Sun   186

Poems by Anjum Wasim Dar
    Do Not Throw Pebbles   188

Poems by Karina Krenn
    We Have Risen So Many Times   190

Poems by Stacy Bannerman
    Empty Boots and Baby Shoes   193
Poems by Nicole Peyrafitte
    Adonis Blue   195
Poems by Georgette Howington
    Haibun for Rice and the Farmers   198
Poems by Cassandra Swan
    The Scorching Stage (They're All Blood Red)   200
    Hitler & the Wayward Shrink   202
Poems by Faleeha Hassan
    Before my friend got killed   206
    My Dangerous Memory   208
Poems by Jane SpokenWord
    Calling 911   210
Poems by Doug Rawlings
    On War Memorials   213
    Walking the Wall   214
    Unexploded Ordnance: A Ballad   215
Poems by Biko Iruti
    Teach Me How to Keep a Woman Happy   217
    Black Butterfly   219
    Down Hill   221
Poems by Amanda Chikomerero Ranganawa
    I Am Happy When I Am Alone   224
    Take Me To The Beach   226
Poems by Catherine Magodo-Mutukwa
    Empty (For Women Who Lost Children)   229
    For Women on the Verge   231
    Home   232

Poems by Mbizo Chirasha

    Empty Dream   234

    Ethiopia   235

    Demons Grazing I   236

    Demons Grazing II   237

    Kongo   237

About the Editors

    Mbizo CHIRASHA   238

    David Swanson   240

About World BEYOND War   242

Introduction by David Swanson

We're trying to overcome a culture of war, a culture that tells people -- and, even more so, shows people through films and novels -- that war is normal. We need a culture of peace, artistic creations that allow us to experience not only living without war, but also what it feels like to be traumatized by danger, damaged by witnessing suffering, permanently altered by killing or by the hatred of those trying to kill. Virtually never in the real world is the horror of war followed by wiping a drop of blood off your lip with the back of your hand and cracking a joke. Nor is the aftermath of war a cheerful commercial break. Nor is permanent preparation for more war anything other than deeply disturbing -- at least not where the wars happen, an area of the earth that has almost no overlap with where weapons are produced.

The poets in this book are from many corners of the globe, a lot of them from places with wars. What does it feel like to be "collateral damage"? Does the violence the world gives you surge past the poverty the world gives you in your list of immediate obsessions, does the violence of war differ from the violence that follows wherever war has been, does the hatred needed for war dissipate faster than the chemicals and radiation, or is it redirected less gruesomely than the cluster bombs? In this book are people who know what war does to the world. They also know and draw references to the popular culture of the places dealing the weaponry and targeting the missiles. They have something to contribute to that culture -- an understanding that war is not an institution to tolerate or respect or refine or glorify, but a sickness to despise and abolish.

Not just abolish. Replace. Replace with compassion, with fellow feeling, with courageous sharing, with a community of peacemakers that is global and intimate, not just honest, not just straight-forward and informed, but inspired and insightful beyond the power of prose or camera. For the pen to have a chance at being mightier than the sword, the poem must be more powerful than the advertisement.

Foreword by Mbizo Chirasha

Mother Earth is broken from incessant decadent wars carelessly perpetuated by mindless, vicious political imbeciles. Our natural wealth plundered by greedy, gluttonous economic dare-devils, imbibing crude oil and fresh blood. Warlord-ism set the suns of our freedom; our earth is torn naked. War is ravaging the beauty of African diamond fields; we are now Wretched Vagabonds. Warlords are frying peace in oil springs of the Gulf. Child Soldiers machete-mutilating innocent wombs in pastures of Sudan. Sons dance to the soprano tune of the gun and sing along to the baritone thud of grenades everyday of God. Xenophobia boiled cousins for a dinner of chopped souls. Somewhere inside the pockets of Africa, the gun throb speaks louder than ballot. Racism and Tribalism are twins gnawing limbs of peace without restraint. Greed buried peace and love in unmarked graves. We rise every dawn with bullets stuck in our rib boxes and horizons weeping blood tears. This global voices collection yearns to expose to utter nudity the evil, cantankerous and devilish shenanigans of ruthless political demigods and cruel-hearted warlords as they incessantly plant wars through their greedy, dictatorial and insatiable quest bloodletting, devilish super-power posturing and unrepentant crude-habit of grabbing natural wealth of both military week and politically fragile countries. It depicts the demise of peace at doorsteps and death of human freedoms as guns smash lives to pulp and wars burn our earth to ashes, due to careless perpetuation by back door political charlatans and uncivilized zealots always bent on polishing the devilish egos of warlords with unwarranted filthy praise. In defiance, we chant resistance, we fist up resilience, we speak peace.

Poems by Ngam Emmanuel

Ty Wasteland

Afternoon, visible rays of the hot sun,
Filtered through the dark grey sky.
The undulating hills overlooked a gritty wasteland below.
The landscape stood imposingly and sullenly, as though
It was been haunted by the witches of melancholy.
Hills that were once carpeted with thick forests
Stood forlorn, empty and weary. Her rugged valleys once
Soared of spectacular beauty. Today her verdant face is no more.
Once, sweet smeliing flowers attracted men and bees here.
Once, the turaco chirped in her lovely woods.
Once, its rapturous melody brought joy to our hearts.
Once, its red shiny feathers graced the crowns of nobility.
Once, the forest provided water for all.
Once, honey dripped abundantly here.
Once, her woods supplied wood for all.
Once, her faune provided cures to all ailments.
Once, the sacred shrines and totems enjoyed its protection.
The gods in their secret places spy and balefully,
Frown at those who neglect the path of the sacred python.
The brooding landscape stares on in disbelief, seeing everyone
Turning its back for pursuit of alien paths.
The defilers of the land increase dailylike raindrops on a drizzling morning.
Blood, spilled at every road junction.
Desecration has stamped wrinkles on every smiling face.
Multitude wander from place to place in quest of solace.
The drummers left behind, play out of tone.
The singers left behind to sing, produce a cacophony.
The dancers left behind to dance, do so awkwardly.

The Wars of Assimilation

Strong swift historical tidal waves
Drifted captors ashore. Shipwrecked
Cruel fate, imprisoned freedom
Stupefied by sunny sandy beaches
Flourish of virgin forest,
Unearthed gems, rich oil wells
Invaders waged a war of conquest.
Thronged into the land with baboonish might,
Consumed by self- importance of full-sized men
carved out a satellite province of Lilliput.
Forced her into a concubinage.
Monarchical kakistocracy implanted.
Strived under grip and whip,
Institutionalising the reign of terror
Coughing out stinking corruption
Lilliputians, transformed into hands,
Tagged contemptuously as brainless
Despised because of origin, language and
Diminutive sizes, accorded second class status.
The monarch to fully dominate, launch,
Wars of assimilation at multiple fronts.
Mental intoxication, falsified curriculum
Smearing youth with sooth of ignorance,
Obstructing the light of true history.
Calculated demolition of structures and institutions,
That made Lilliput famous and proud.
Siphon of rich oil wells, leaving people thirsty
And hungry. Desert encroaching due to
Wanton butchery of virgin forest.

Pent-up frustrations, ignited flames of liberty,
hatching persistent uproars,
shaking fragile foundation of a loose
Incompetent corrupt monarchy.
Trepidation in the silver palace
King in precipitation unleashes
egregious lethal crackdown on divorcees.
Satellite transformed into battlefield.
War machines intone dirges as they
swallow of up fleeing souls. Whimpers
Of pain submerged by its pounding.
Manned birds fart bombs and bullets.
Infantry loots, rapes, kills and roasts villages
Armed groups crop up daily
Conflict grows bigger
Death toll on the rise
Journey to freedom bloodier,
The world watching in sadistic approval.
The wheels of progress on a stand still.

Ascension Thursday

As you go up to the heavens dear Lord,
Sprinkle unto this desolate land thy mystical colors,
Standing crestfallen, flooded by bloodbath,
Smitten by violent strife and hate.
Let the mystery in these colors
Absorb the awful sights of war.
Let this Mystical fragrance,
Perfume our broken hearts
Let thy mystical presence
Silence the whizzing bullets
stop the pounding of war machines
healing overburdened hearts.
Let thy mystical strength
Melt away teary eyes of
Grieving souls who've lost
all in sizzling flames
Let the mystery in this colors bring
Healing to the oppressed, who
depressed, see their sun slipping
sleepily away over the horizon.
Let thy mysterious tidings
Intone new songs in our hearts
Let men hear now with their hearts
Take us through this tunnel of pain
to enjoy the spoils of peace.

When the Election Approaches

The Pharisee spends blank nights.
Countless manipulative strategies spiraling
the web of his corrupt mind. With messianic zeal this
Sanctimonious political bootlicker combs countryside nooks
in flashy limousines as if to mock the foot users.
Bearer of nude promises of hope, fussy of rival's activities,
resorts to stage fake shows of fame to canvass support.
Mesmerizes local populace with temporal tranquilizers.
Resolute to remain up there, while the wretched down here.
Election fever attains pitch, his melody becomes mellower,
His tongue sweeter, his attitude humbler.
In a hurly-burly of a political party, the plaster saint
magically entrances the bewildered masses with a litany of envisaged projects.
Dust settles on hope, vicious cycle restarts on the rails of stagnation.
Catapulted to glory, he turns eyes to the skies.
Ghetto dwellers rehearse same songs of sorrow.
Wallow in mud of poverty, smiles buried in high mortality.
Heath, education, economy depreciate in the wicked hands of greed and self-interest.
Roads remain death traps. The downtrodden licks deep wounds of deception.

Ngam Emmanuel is a poet, writer, advocate of political justice, and high school teacher in Cameroon. Ngam graduated from Higher Teacher Training College with a Diploma in Languages (French and English).

Poems by Jambiya Kai

Pokerman

If you play your hand in the hope of sensual offers of success, ponder the false imagery of hope
and indulge superficial calls of happiness, then that god owns a part of you.
It is mammon's mental games that hold you captive as he webs a band of restlessness tightly around your desires and draws you in, one glowing sceptre at a time.
a god that manipulates your nutrition.
your dwelling place,
your habitation.
Chains of bondage dragging you inside the mangy walls of dark and damp dungeons from which you can be saved.
Yet you will never be free
if you appraise a crafty warlord;
bound by your inner rebellion and secret nurturing of what should be burnt and banished.
Stop sharing space with the dead from which you should run;
find no pleasure in popcorn peace
lest you be submerged in a sticky abyss of no return.
As a dog returns to its vomit so is the man who puts his hand to the plough and looks back;
a mere salt encrusted figurine mounted in mid air,
the shrine of a soul who refuses to let the warmonger go.
Such is the nature of mammon's games –
The fiendish fashion icon.
If you play often enough it will drive a stake through your heart and own your soul; slit your throat and leave you bleeding.
Disengage from the possessed materialist;

from the "Fuhrer" who promises bread but gives a stone.
Disregard leaders who steal your meal.
Stop the games,
protect the back of your brother;
Join him in the firing line –
be the media spine,
and together you must cry,
"This is my living space,
my country,
My home –
This is,
"My Struggle".

The Secret Society

It was an ear-splitting slap.
Her head bounced off the wall and hit the floor with a thud
His dentures slipped to the corners of puffy lips;
The stench of fermented mash all too familiar.
Whack
Swish
Boom!
Ribs
Lips
Broken
Cracked
Size 12's with split soles
working boots of a disgruntled man
Frills and polka dots were stained with bourbon and blood;
Her bruised blue eyes traced the coffee stains along the wall,
her ponytail he yanked till her scalp bled
The mother of 2 was dragged from kitchen to bedroom,
to be a wife.
The phone screamed into the bloody fight.
The male voice bleeped confidently -
"You have reached the home of Reverend Simons and his family.
We are not available but please leave your number............"
Snores reverberate through whisky breath.
Everything goes bump in the night
Broken, Broken
Reverend Simons and his family were broken.
Katy slipped her battered body out of bed and limped to the study where
she would prayerfully guard her sacred secret -
Pain split her head like a lightning bolt
Tomorrow they would bind her wounds as they had always done for the

past years....
conspirators they were -
The dentist, The Doctor
And the Reverend.
They were all, broken.
But some stories are best kept hidden –
for a broken home, like Katy's home
was better than no home at all.
Upstairs 7 year old Melissa snuggled close to her big sister -
"Don't cry Mandy, I will pray for you,
maybe God will send us help", she whimpered.
The sun yawned into a new day;
Little Melissa placed a single rose over her mother's buried secret
The night claimed Katy's life.
Beside her shattered dreams
The dentist and the doctor,
the Reverend and his congregation
lift their voices in solemn praise –
"Nearer my God to Thee", they sing.*
Nearer to thee – "
Though like a wanderer
the sun gone down
darkness comes over me -
my rest a stone;
yet in my dreams I'd be
nearer to Thee.
What a Holy night
when reverend Simon took Katy's life –
A heart attack they said.
On Sunday he will preach,
"We miss our Katie".
And the congregation will mourn
And weep with guilt.

"What a Pretty Boy" – The Story of Juneck Livi

We were caught in a civil war – the mob petrol bombed our home in a township in South Africa.
I was just five years old with no idea of the terror that raged outside my home.
The faction fighting and brandishing arms were displays of bitterness that ignited and flared into a towering inferno – I was the innocent victim and those who fought to rid their town of "traitors" were unaware that they had obliterated their aims when their flamed torches clung to my skin. To my home.
but then again, there are no victors in war.
And men give their lives for freedom.
The scars were deep and skin grafting my second home throughout high school.
When the students refused to listen my teacher would make his point , "Don't you bunch listen – are your ears glued like Juneck's"? In those few words I heard the hiss of the blue-gum slats that framed our home and hypnotically watched as the pomegranate flames hungrily devoured my young flesh. In my teacher's taunt I melted into screams. I found solace in the songs of sirens as I fought the inevitable.

I was only 5 but trauma slept like an idolised mummy. Ferocious in worship. Memories of my mother were vague. The Beautiful Angolan jazz singer Maria Livi was sharp-witted and humorous but there was no miracle at hand when a contaminated blood transfusion emptied her life. Hers was the only photograph that survived the fires of hell. My short life lay scattered among the debris. Perhaps she was keeping me sane from the earth below my twisted misshapen feet. Or was it from the heaven's above my tell-tale scalp.

My father and stepbrother's lived in another province –
I was a reminder of the sins of life and one they did not want around. My grandmother died that fateful night when the rioters set our town alight. I never told my counselor how I saw her skin shrivel and peel away as she wrapped her arms around me – her eyes loving me when I was 5 years old and quite handsome in her embrace. Until she could no longer hold onto me.

Her heart would be broken if she knew that despite her best efforts I no longer look like the "pretty boy" she loved. Maybe she knows. Aunty Aya was a good mother to me and I was blessed to have mothers who showed me the light of love.

My marred face and disabled hands became the butt of everyone's joke and the mockery followed me around –

I was ostracised and beaten by the same ones who fought for my freedom; who plundered the system for my liberty.

Who burnt my home, killed my guardian angel and massacred my dreams. Like sheep to the slaughter.

Despite my adversities, my faith sustained me; my grandmother's sacrifice and dying words helped me to move past the pain of bullying, past the stigma of "ugly".

"No matter what Juneck", she screamed and coughed across, through and above the crashing timber, and the fiery serpent that sucked at her throat, "don't let the cruelty of this world steal the beauty of your dreams". Her hands circled my face as if to ward off the blazing demon. Gold eyes and sizzling red mouth spitting all over my 5 year old face. The god that haunted my every waking moment.

The devil lived inside mirrors. I wished I had died in the lunacy. In the fight for freedom. Wishing the angry mob had killed me

If only the menacious bullies would know the horror of the scourged,

the savagery of skin dripping from one's face – like the terrifying lick of a dragon's searing tongue – while a ruthless grenade lay your life asunder.

I was just 5 then. 40 Years ago.

I have since embraced my own beauty, and my soul has been exorcised from purgatory.
I will not imitate the society that had dealt so treacherously with me –
I had determined that despair would not hold me ransom. That I would be free, for I knew where my help came from;
my strength.
My purpose.
My grandmother's hope was mine.
Beyond the mountains and the hills I lifted my voice and my prayers were answered.
In this shaky journey love carries me above my storms.
I smile into a mirror and see God there.
My eyes illuminated with love
There is no ugly in me –
My grandmother loved me at 5 when i was a pretty boy.
Now I am a handsome soul
A man who walked through fire,
reeking of victory
This world is not my home.
One day I too, like my grandmother,
shall be completely whole.
I no longer hear the hiss of the blue-gum slats through shameful words but the sound of the abundance of rain in my grandmother's screams across, through and above the falling timber and fiery serpent that sucked at her throat,
"No matter what Juneck, don't let the cruelty of this world steal the beauty of your dreams".
I was loved at 5 when I was a pretty boy.
I'm richer than I was then.
For now I am loved by the man in the mirror
And the woman who holds my hand when the blue gum slats sometimes come crashing down around me.

Notes

"Katy's Secret" is a work of fiction based upon real documented incidences.
* "Nearer my God to Thee" is taken from a hymn written by Sarah Flower Adams.
"What a Pretty Boy" is a story shaped around real events and a real hero who touched my heart.

Jambiya Kai is an emotive writer and storyteller from South Africa who weaves the tragedy and victory of the human experience into a tapestry of memorable imagery and metaphor. She speaks with honesty on the socio-spiritual challenges of our time.

Poems by Sydney Saize

Dry Cry

Cleanse the blood that stained Chimoio
Heal the bleeding wounds of those bruised in Chitungwiza
Respect their affiliation
Is it still Rhodesia that you forward with the land act
Draft the tears of homeless Manzou residents
Evicted
Evitated
Savages' expansion
Exploitation
Victimization
Industrializing our piece of earth
What's that worth?
Citizens turned to destitutes
Morden day fruit-gatherers
And cave-dwellers
Our vote displaced us
Only mountains are shielding our salvage
How long shall people bleed?
Citizens weep
Cry blood Zimbabwe its revolution time
The hour is at hand
Dictatorial sun must set
Justice and freedom day dawn
Tired of wet cheeks
Dry cry the world can't see
Soldier up no more turn cheek
This time let us not bow down.

A Dilema

Patience doesn't pay
But only averts in a way
For they preach what they ignore to practice
And the reality remains of milking dry the victims
They swear and their vows are perjury
How I wish if I was a jury?
To roast this detriment
Those who are crying
Are recompensed with utmost pain
Those who creates awareness
And defends, justly
Are marginalized
And sacrificed on the cross
Like Christ nailed innocent
Only filthying the altar
So I beg you to rise to the occasion
Let's fiercely expel them like demons
Another Chimurenga that drove the Smith regime
Of patriotic regiments
Driven with the passion for justice and a competent governance Patience doesn't pay
For years we have been patiently waiting
But only in vain
Promises comforted us
Then scourged us as fool
The nation is in dire straits

Shame

We sympathized shame
Brought it on the table to discuss
Our groaning hearts confined to bleed
Simulating hilarity faces
A nation pulverized
Economic models evolving to rip the poor citizens
Political bigger heads living wantonly
Shamelessly neglecting voices of a suffering mass
Parading ego to revel their victims in applause
Shame, left me dazzed
With my pen bleeding ink
Vomiting impetus forces of victory
A mind in my story
Dictators I'm sorry
For expressing my worry
Worries of a real revolution
A change of cir' es not persons
Both partisans and peasants eating alike
Not only when the cow piss the shit the farmer jubilates
People needs food in their plates
Rallies and propaganda ain't our production
The effects are now embedding in our DNA.

The Liberty They Were Denied

The streets that we walk
in frivolous garbs
with our lovely family and friends
is the same streets that are nurturing abandoned children
Children who are homeless
Destitute
and hungry
The food that we call leftovers
and we deliberately through away in a rubbish bit
in Durban Street
and High Street
are but delicacies
for them who are starving
The money that you rob the poor
can you give it away for charity
to rescue a terrified society
of children who survived the burns
the flames
the fire
That stole their beauty
their comeliness
Their imbue
their liberty
their confidence
To have them ripped
robbed
and raped.

Ghetto Bulletins

The news leaflets I digested
on child molestation
And human trafficking
Have vomited this fuss
a fiery ghetto bulletin
of tender fruits yield before time
Stillbirth of bitter before ripe, ready and sweet
Tampered plants before they pollinate and bloom
The future becomes bleak
Heartless bastards are ill-spending
insinuating the dollar value
on smuggling human bodies
as commodities for sale
kidnapping them without a family's farewell
Streets are turned into danger zones
Gangsters perambulating to lodge our bosoms in fear
Oh dear
The streets are bloody
Tearful victims unpaid
and underpaid underage vicinage
This spiracle should be consummated
To suffocate these criminals
into incarceration

Dry Season

In this dry season
We sow hope
To reap thorns and thistles
Mother poking children
Jab the nation to starvation
Sickening the nation with confusion
Their corruption
The victims of elections
Are ready for the coming polls
Ridiculous
Its a pity we are like adopted children
Now only my mind is what I consider divine
What I know all promises are so blossoming
But fulfilling them is not a bed of rose
Can't fool the youth with yesterday's delights
It's high time the ground need cultivation
Societies are weeping over transformation
Revolution or reformation

The Syntactics of a Regime

Babylon is a system
depriving citizens of their basic rights
to cast them in a dungeon
just to create a piece of shit called politics
synthetic of rhetoric's
And semantics
Namely propaganda and slogans
polished morphemes fashioned to mean smiles on screw faces
Babylon is a paradox
of learned cuckoos
Who voice void promises
only to rape intellectual capacity of the suffering mass
a people vulnerable to both internal
And external power struggles
struggles of power hungry cowards
who onslaught a nation to satisfy their greedy
Babylon is a cyanogen of paramount paragons
who reacts to propell frustrations
starvation
and deaths of innocent soul
Dangerous rebels in suits
Experts in homicide
Suicide
and Economicides
Babylon is here
Babylon is there
Babylon is everywhere
Babylon is continuous
Babylon is contagious
Babylon is them rigging votes in a peaceful election
Babylon is when you vote but for no avail.

Sydney Saize is a socio-political commentator from Zimbabwe piercing the heart of misrule, maladmistration, corruption, and injustice. He narrates the political ills and suffers the consequences.

Poems by Wilson Waison Tinotenda

Voices from the Ashes

I
Note that I was murdered to have risen transformed
Note that my flesh and blood was readily made dust
Note that my bones and skeletons got incriminated
Note that my impetuous voice echoes from the ashes
Note how I was silenced... to have risen transformed
Note how I struggled: from the liberation coercion
Note how I triumphed over the sceptre and bayonets
Note how I gamed over the war sceneries impeccably
II
Note that I was flawless, efficient, resilient, competent
Note that my energies were sapped during the event
Note that my knee crawled from valley to valley deep
Note that my aim was for the betterment of the kins
Note how I was enslaved* before and fought swiftly
Note how I become a guerrilla in motherland, savage
Note how I ruptured apart the foes and the schemes
Note how I became violent and vigilant in my domain
III
Note that I was a victor before I got engraved deeply
Note that my wrath did grew with the evolution peak
Note that my beloved comrade back stabbed his own
Note that my bones has risen the ashes mould vessels
And let my long gone blood reflow from the pool of
That Impetuous distant rivers, and rekindle the lost
Blazing flames of the Chimurenga wars... Magamba

Josiah Tongogara the barracks named after decades
IV
Denote when I rise from the ashes I votes mercilessly
Denote when my passions gather I will spit of venom
Denote when my strengths grew I will fight back fists
Denote when my courage reverberates I will burst out
Denote when I become potent, I will reign over again
Denote when I am with the mighty I will aside favours
Denote when I reign the Augustus house it will report
Denote when I speak order will reign, reconstructions
V
Denote how the muddled economy will reboot again
Denote how the incubators of corruption will vanish
Denote how the lost zealous and confidence bestow
Denote how the ills and evils will be driven to extinct
Denote how the brothers will cheer from the drums
Denote how the sisters will break a leg to Jerusalem
Denote how the fathers will fail conscience off brew
Denote how the mothers will pail the yeild in joyous

Fear

Raised in harmony and tranquillity, from infancy
Never was I poised between these storms that's
Disillusionment and Disparity, tolls in prevalence
Childhood being and been a bliss, gone by blast
Hell on earth is the odds, a sour bite of truths
so savage and raves the minds a milestone away
Escapism votes my fate through veto, sad thots
Derived each second of this phase of livelihood.
Once the brave diva that raised an innocent son
Descendant to the wise crown tore apart the tires
readily a nob that had been strained and fragile
to have pulled the string all will point vehemently.
What shall it became this lifeless experience cast
Fist upon fist, pound of flesh bled... oozes blood
Stained be the cordial relation strained due to...
Due to... These episodes brought about my fears.

Before the black man's turmoil was his foster
And race amongst them was an imposter too
No wonder I grew to watch from a black and
White television set... from infancy to juvenile
Ages had past, each day break Ma got rinsed
Busking became a hobby... Never was I eager
To question the brother's ill treat, I grew too,
To acknowledge his inflictions and incursions
Now that I had proudly waved the colonial fleet
As the show got clear and clearer, letting off
By-gones be by-gones another race was being
Bred... Blackism rose. Brothers upon brothers.

The spirit of Madhibha never sort Xenophobia
Zulu ramps BaShona, Mfecane of the 21st century
Africa now a war zone tribe against tribe awry...
Nehanda was this your plight Ma?

Wilson Waison Tinotenda is a poet and flash fiction writer from Zimbabwe, the editor of Deem.lit.org and its founding father. A human rights activist, an ardent follower of the Zimbabwe We Want campaign and currently a Student at Open Learning Centre studying Accounting.

Poems by Aleck T Mabenge

Burnt

When life dealt me its cards I got burned;
New dawn new era;
To be celebrated not, for every day in the mirror I am reminded;
The pain, the hurt, the why me in every scar;
Marks of the unfairness of life as for me fire decided;
Flames screaming burn, child burn, but I survived.
The fuel of that pain only the universe knows;
How and why, I can't say;
Friends I had, turned into foes;
Dreams of an even skin, even only when with others I play;
It is not love but pity that had them open their doors;
Pity or love, I survived.
Fire the instrument my poverty;
I hate that You and me are bound for life;
Bound with creams and medication, my only property;
Fire I hate you but can't live without you my wife,
We intimately mingled and tangled as me you burned,
This skin of mine you robbed,
But strength in my soul you forged,
I SURVIVED!

Aleck T Mabenge of Zimbabwe is a passionate poet who writes for the love of poetry and as a way to have his voice heard on a broad range of issues. His poetry is influenced by the socio-econo-political issues of the day world-wide. His hope is that his message reignites the dream of our fathers of a prosperous, peaceful Zimbabwe whose people look forward to a brighter future free of social ills, disease, and injustice.

Poems by Tshepo Phokoje

Fear

Oh, your presence is paralyzing, those multiple mental battles you have won.
Your ugly cousin doubt, jubilantly announcing your arrival, but who invited you here?
You infiltrate homesteads and nations alike; your roots have dug deep into innocent souls.
How long will our people have to endure your bitter fruits?
You are the ice-cold behind the feet of a bride-to-be, causing her to flee the alter
Scared of a future with no forecasted honeymoons.
You know that she left behind a man with a bruised ego and shattered dreams?
You stood there watching another series of dreams evaporating into the sky
As you shamelessly flashed your toothless grin, doing your victory dance.
You quietly sneaked into my Timbuktu's yard, into her son's mind
He was dismissed from a meager job, but all he could see was you, disguised as the end
You told him that he was done for, about how useless he was
And he was found hanging from the poles of his mother's hut
With her favorite doek tied around his young neck.
If you were a color, you would be an ugly shade of grey, black glazing for a glossy touch
As you wear your cloak of pride adorned with spikes and thorny bits
You walk around carrying a box full of blades as you destroy the flesh on your way in and out
The discomfort that you are, heart pounding, sweaty palms and a mouth as dry as the Kalahari

A blackout later, after you have sucked the light out of a burning spirit.
A jealous lover beats his woman to a pulp for wanting to leave, the love died, she wanted out.
You whispered to him, "
Another man is going to touch her delicate skin, kiss the lips you have kissed, eat from the same plate you ate in" and he believed you.
If he couldn't have her, no one else would, her blood on his hands, splashed on his white shirt, a canvas of pain and regret, but it was too late.
He will spend the rest of life running, from himself.

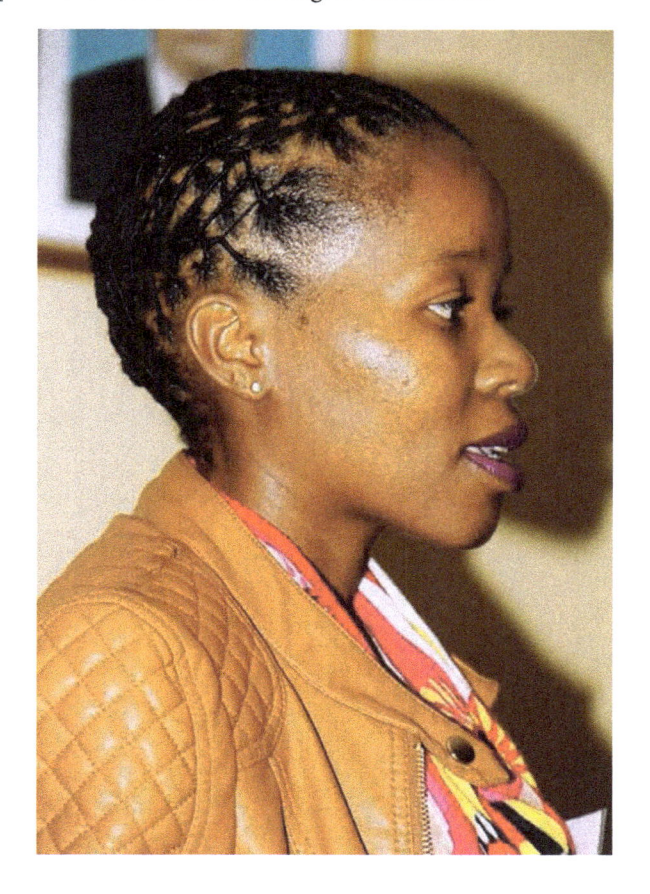

Tshepo Phokoje is a poet, writer, and human rights activist from Botswana.

Poems by Alan Britt

Africa

(For George Nelson Preston)

Hungry, as in haven't eaten for days,
weeks, belly full of scorpions
from insults hurled like grenades.
The League of Nations reincorporated,
but the new League of Nations has a budget
that doesn't include my bursting belly;
the new League of Nations has bigger
fish to fry; meanwhile my belly full
of Aunts, Uncles, Cousins,
& distant birth parents doesn't
qualify me for the neediest continent
on this planet.
Their vision.
Not mine.

Alan Britt, of the United States, has published over 3,000 poems nationally and internationally.

Poems by Richmore Tera

Child of the Struggle

I was born within the struggle
amidst glowing embers
Raging fires
and screams that threatened to tear the sky apart.
They named me Struggle.
I grew up with the struggle
and the struggle took me to other struggles.
With my namesakes
also called Struggle
We obliged, for that was the only way we could survive the struggle
and its other struggles.
Now we are in another struggle
Where struggles are the order of the day
And no matter how much I struggle
Still I can't erase my name Struggle
From my birth certificate
For that is what I am –
A child of the struggle.

Desideratum

you're our desideratum
every corner we scour
with hungry eyes
hopping for your power
for your shower
on the parched skin of our lives

Samosa Town

Gone from my town is the one-cent coin,
Miniature wheels rolled into the tunnels of oblivion
By the fickle hands of mounting inflation.
Remember how it looked like?
Then I will reward you with a dollar
To buy yourself a sweet cake.
The datum line now is the ten cent-coin
Not a cent as in the days of yore.
Anything less than ten cents
Earns you disdainful looks
From the peevish vendors on the streets.
Ten cents, the price of a samosa.
Samosa that won't fill your belly
But melts in your mouth like warm butter
Leaving a tangy after-taste
Of congealed oil on your hankering tongue.
Samosa made from dough
Kneaded from flour
Past its best-before date,
Spices filched from the local bazaar,
Rotten potatoes, tomatoes and peas
Picked from the market dumpsite,
Baked in used oil
Over a fire from disused car-tyres
On the banks of the turbid Mukuvisi River.
And every little thing takes after the samosa:
Sweets - ten cents for two;
Need a smoke - then part with your ten cents;
Box of matches - ten cents,
Single banana - ten cents.

If your bus-fare is short with ten cents
Then you stand in the overcrowded aisle
While the haves with dollars to spare
Nudge you in the ribs from the comfort of their seats.
Want to enquire about directions?
Upfront you ought to have ten cents.
Ten cents and upwards
So is the trend of the prices for everything
In this samosa town
Where the one cent-coin
Now is history
In the books of economics.

Richmore Tera was a poet, short story writer, playwright, actor, and freelance journalist who once worked for Zimpapers (writing for *The Herald, Sunday Mail, Kwayedza, Manica Post, H-Metro*) as a reporter but later focusing on his creative work.

Poems by Vanessa KaluKWETE

70 Years Younger

Youth hood discovered me in my grey years,
As gaze flipped my world upside down,
As i traveled down the memory lane,
I obliterate the joys of aging
As a stream of tears trickled down my cheeks.
A bubbling cauldron of images,
breeds tendrils and strands,
Appearing as random images;
Dreams strike a chord in my mind,
Brewing a mixture of pain and regret,
Regret over the "virgin heart"
A migraine pummels louder,
Fighting with a sense of nausea ,
Only then do i let the memories sublime,
As they sour perception of self;
Making "self" look inferior
I resort to living in the moment as i embrace FATE.

Backyard

I have yearned to see its beauty,
To view its epic formation
As I lie in the euphoria of wishes,
Dreams have been the stand,
The stand i have leaned on
As I reside in its vacuum.
I have fallen a thousand times,
But still I have failed to get up;
I have longed to see a glimpse of my face,
Decipher what "others" call beauty and ugliness
But within the confinements of my emotional organ,
Lies shattered pieces of agony
Most of it all I have loved
As I have fallen in love with scents and sounds;
But what I have to regain is my optical nature,
As I lie in my own backyard.

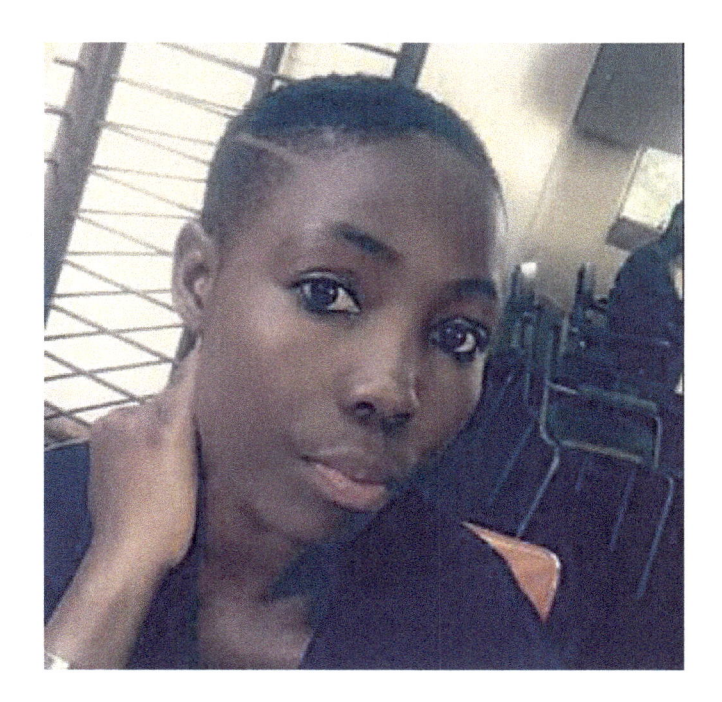

Vanessa KaluKWETE is studying Psychology at the University of Zimbabwe. She is a poetry fanatic and enjoys reading novels.

Poems by Chrispah Munyoro

Vultures in Disguise

The sprouting of life.
Began in darkness.
Conquering the malice of the evil.
Oh----stay alive ----dear child.
Inspire of where you are breathing.
Nobody to play with.
Without toys to amuse you.
A loner, kicking the unseen.
A recluse moving alone.
Your actions in pitch darkness.
Gives hopes, wishes, happiness.
Breathing you are, active you are.
Dear child, a source of jubilee to your parents.
Pride as you grow big.
Even though the loving mother is worried.
Loses shape like a drunkard addicted to traditional brewed beer.
Most of the time mother being sick.
Eating the unpalatable.
The father working tirelessly.
Oh ---for you ----precious child.
Gruesome pains for your journey.
Out of darkness into light.
Waters, sweat, tears and blood shed.
In some cases even loss of life.
For the transformation to the world.

Hell! A high price to be paid.
Your battle with life and death.
Squashing dark spirits, becoming a warrior.
Ululations, tears of joy greeting you.
Welcoming you child from the unknown.
If only you knew!
You would had stayed in that lonely world.
For the glittery you see would be like Hades.
The freshness of the world will suffocate you.
The celebrations of your arrival.
Oh ----dear child ----will be sorrow.
Tenderness to be replaced by anguish.
Lingering are the unfeeling vultures.
Waiting to devour your life.
Greedy destroying your future.
Vampires sucking all emotions.

Blasting of Explosives

The richness oozing.
Magnetic attracting deadly sting.
The soil breathing winter of June.
Underneath gems pilling like dune.
Sprouting and arranged as a pyramid.
Of which flesh blood soaks them amid.
Africa so loaded and on the top of the pose.
Like a star, always there shining engraved with pompous.
The unbelievable, when it blasts the fire in the moss.
Spreading bad odour, poisonous to the mass.
Gem panniers in the greatest zone of war.
Which leaves souls at confused par?
The golden pieces a scent of death.
Once upon a time, it was a myth.
Today death is ululated like a celebration.
For grabbing the gems is a marathon.
The survival of the fittest is the game.
Robbing life cunningly without shame.
Africa with the bitterness of paprika.
Widows, orphans, friends crying without a breaker.
Fathers, brothers, sisters all swiped off.
By the careless, blasting and unfeeling oaf.
Death for the ore.
Registered pain for all.
The copperplate dressed by human fresh blood.
Coldly salivating the raucous mood.
Stamp mill singing songs crashing bones.
Of the bright future stolen and swiftly bygones.
The more they perish.
In the mirror of life greatness perish.

Black Opal

The molasses type of skin.
Created with the coating of honey.
So preserved to the core.
With the scent of best blooms.
Fixated by the enhancing spices.
Very tolerant to weather conditions.
Blessed with the sun.
Baking the skin to tan.
Winds fail to chap it.
In the cold it will be sweating.
Cicadas and birds making melodious mellow.
God's best ever creation.
The black color, the black skin.
Rise up black, rise!
Illuminated by the stars.
Caressed by lovely fresh breeze.
Enchanting, the moon always lingers.
Wanting to dance in the black skies.
The darker the most.
The dawn is so nearer.
Doves in a sing-song.
Crows crowing to welcoming the new day.
The dew, sweetly sprayed on the plants.
It's a new day.
From gory to glory.
A blessing to black people.
Shedding off calories naturally.
Bathing in sweat to maintain,
The masculine and forever youthful skin.

Munching the abundant fruits.
Full of nature's sweetness.
Enjoying vegetables,so essential to health.
Harvesting them and sun-dried.
Great forests full of salivating delicacy, wild animals.
Without too much fats.
That endangers the health.
In the homestead plenty and more.
Livestock, goats, chickens, pigeons, rabbits.
The list goes on.
Just grows naturally.
As the creator intended them to be.
Flawless, shiny, precious as the best gems.
Which are flourishing under your feet.
A paradise on earth.
A place where every being wishes for.
Bathing in streams, rivers.
Natural jacuzzis, bathtubs and swimming pools.
With your hard working expect hands.
Competing with best machinery.
Powerhouses of great wealth.
Black color, black skin.
Warriors, withstanding many hurdles.
Full of intellects.
Adore you, respect you, cherish you.
Treasure you, salute you.
Black opal skin.

Delis Uproar

The genius unstable with schizophrenia
Universe blemished by great mania
Suffering from dementia.
Sprouting vigorously them lunatics
Living with serenity in antics
The minds erased of humanity ethics.
Like the brewery bursting with beer
Flabbergasted worldwide in deep fear
Bracing the strong antipathy of xenophobia.
The clock wildly being rebellious
Hens with racquets throwing their eggs leaving mess
The sun raising from the west, sinking in the east.
Black and white signing to merge
Youths graduating as drunkards
Elders always raucous.
Wild animals escaping locked cage
Finding peace on the horrendous edge
With no-one to capture
Even taking a picture
Good and bad in a strange mixture
Gleefully waiting for the rapture.

Chrispah Munyoro is a student of Applied Art and Design, Graphics and Website Programming at Kwekwe Polytechnic College in Zimbabwe. Munyoro is a talented writer, journalist and a dedicated Design Artist. She is natural linguist, fluent in many languages.

Poems by Geraldine Sinyuy

Elegy for My Brother

Jump, how could you do this to me?
Emma, little bro, can you see me?
Do you also weep this sudden separation?
Emmanuel, what I kept for you,
That parcel I have longed prepared in my mind,
Your own share of the fruits of
My toil in the world of knowledge,
Has remained but a dream.
Emma, you mocked at me.

My plans, brother, are frozen,
Frozen by the sudden seizure
Of that breath that gave you life.

Brother, you went silently like a stranger.
You did not leave a word for me.
Jump, your absence slaps me on the face.
My shoulders have fallen,
for I hold no more pride of a brother!
Emma, now I speak in retrospectives:
"We were..."
Yes, that is the tense your departure has left me with!

Geraldine Sinyuy (PhD), is from Cameroon. In 2016, she performed one of her poems entitled "On a Lone and Silent Hill" during an International Conference on World Environment Day at Imo State University, Nigeria.

Poems by Chad Norman

The Flagless Flagpole

Today I can't care about
the intrusive news of the world,
and I can't care about
the life of a younger man seated
beside a bench I enjoy as the finches
share songs with a sun I can't care about,
only use as a hope to warm the back
of my neck where the wind
remains cold under the collar
I leave open in order to not care about
the stranger walking by, asking
himself, along with the wind and sun,
"Do you really think I am stupid?"

At this point in the bike-ride home
I can't care about the chem-trail
left in the blue sky above us, an
us I want to care about
only if we begin to take the time
seated out in the open where
we can be seen, bald-heads, ball-caps
on backwards and forwards,
burkas, niqabs, hijabs, turbans, etc., all we use to adorn or admit to
ourselves this is who I must be,
this is what I follow, what I believe in
if you will, what I wear allows a
tiny look into the self I am trying

to keep sacred, but what I wear
is meant to hide nothing other than
what we all were told to keep hidden,
boy and girl, man and woman.

Today I want to care about one thing,
a longing to be a Canadian...
being born here, or having had
the courage to choose this country
and somehow find the way,
to eventually stay on some land,
some perfect selected property.
You will soon own, soon call
a piece of the planet your new home.

Where the Path Is Melting

How quiet can a child be?

Please, please, bury me
with Hope Sandoval singing,
"In To Dust"
as the singer of Mazzy Star,
as the world becomes more bizarre.

How quiet can a man be?

Thank you, thank you, hear me
with only these words,
my words, no famous singer,
just me, saying these lines,
just the world ignoring the poet.

It is day now, so daylight talks,
in among all the voices of Winter
lodged where cold isn't a brute,
but when I recall that child
asking for so little when so little
I love how much I don't know,
I don't want to know.

Done with the branches' strengths
you come up the driveway
with perfect legs, playing yourself
through strings and power
left to a song you know I know.

The one left of where the pen sat, yes,
over in the drawer you protect
where the child & man have laughed
over and over because life gives
of course, gives each one a bit
of daylight and darkness.

Something someone will find
out in the middle of a field
where snow drifts over old footprints.

The melting path of all planning
to leave homelands being bombed
or lied to, taken from their children
they believe Canada can help raise,
can help to get to the other side
where a piece of clear ground is found.

No snow, no wind, no opposition
to them simply hoping
to stand and not slip on
any wish to have them fall.

Chad Norman lives beside the high-tides of the Bay of Fundy, Truro, Nova Scotia. He has given talks and readings in Denmark, Sweden, Wales, Ireland, Scotland, America, and across Canada. His poems appear in publications around the world and have been translated into Danish, Albanian, Romanian, Turkish, Italian, and Polish.

Poems by James Coburn

Damnation

Pieces missing from your reptilian heart
pressing on a man pleading for breath.
No breath will ever revive George Floyd.

"Momma" he cried.
What happened to make you so unconscionable
to force the life out a man
with the weight of injustice
pulling humanity's roots?

What have you done,
but to level a child of God
in a pool of death
as you look the other way.

Some days cry hard enough
to flood the earth.
Now you enter my night
but his light shines,
and I see you for what you are.

Crossing the Bridge

Before his walk across Brooklyn Bridge,
faces and conversation
left no impression.
No bridge builders high in wind
absorbed sound, felt raindrops,
or linked exteriors throughout the city.
He lived a life of indifference.

Beams of steel, intransigent
as a settled past, lost pace
in atoms fixed in matter.
Never did an artist's eye
collect impressions of a crowd
in motion.
Not a brush stroke, at least for him.
Footsteps lagged from an heroic day.
They penetrated not even a thought
beyond his last conversation.

Lending a Hand

When our youngest are crushed
with lapse of breath —
due to nature or misguidance
or a hand never lent,
there a time question
why take innocence away.

When children die at borders
betrayed by harm's way;
we are the hemisphere of silence,
lost until kindness comes in play.

Before a Queen's condolences at Aberfan
or rescue workers sift through an air strike,
we hear the cry of a child
hasten shadow to light.

As footsteps bring bullets to side with fear
we inhale the Almighty to carry us near
the thatched villages, places of home.
When love is spoken, we're never alone.

James Coburn is an Oklahoma poet in the United States of America. Coburn has always valued the subtext of life and seeks to reveal its undercurrents. He believes indifference is the enemy of man as it is the benefactor of ignorance, racism and xenophobia. Coburn is currently collaborating with Nairobi poet Brian Kasaine on a book of poetry.

Poems by Sadiqullah Khan

May I Ask

For am grieved to the marrow -
That be if a child play, - you sold -
Worse than in slavery, the ones
Picked and stolen from mothers' laps
Every name is lost every missing dead -
Did you trade in them, may I ask?
This is not a poetic hyperbole without sub-
Stance. This is your statistical head count.
Sold or killed is your reply, and the homeless?
The immeasurable suffering and forfeiture
Honour, citizens' rights and law?
I turn my face this way and that
It's the same sight everywhere -
There are graveyards spread over miles
A sneaking author once said
Who stole herself through the biggest
Prison on earth where inmates suffocate
Or breathe in the destruction you brought.

Thus Plunged Deeper

And the haze she was -
Write me a bio of her
Or for me
Press the search button
For me to know -
The high is 'ice',
Or popularity's fall
That was too early, these -
Unless enough spiritualized
In their dark maze lost -
Thus plunged deeper
And deeper -
Law of diminishing return
Wanting, they impossible
Assigning fears on others -
For they know not
That from a rise there is fall
Without anybody's mistake
The quick rapid fame
You stair upon
May be a quicker descent
Or it may be a right
Freedom speakers are giants
As adamant to destroy
Dissent and plain freedom -
As tyrant falls upon the innocent
Or she not knowing
In real world who protect
Rabbits are called chickens

And have therefore
To put a patient fight up.
- On Nasim Najafi Aghdam
- Conversation with George T. Everette

Oppressive Society

Paulo Friere Series III
Go to their schools with Friere checklist -
Find out the level of oppression
Although extendable spherically
En-circumference all offices
Many a home - and much more,
Authoritarian respect for authority
No matter repressive - the conduct
Conform and you are hypocritical -
In streak find out with this check list
Which better by heart memorise
To place them or yourself
In equation this though is so rampant
Of ethos part in body politic
Or social mores and global polity
The big cop and tin-pot general
Defaced bureaucrat worthless politician

An Inauguration

He, the politician inaugurates -
They clap, - softly then vigorously -
What a claim on their lives
Drinking water from hand pump,
A blue ribbon is cut with new scissor -
Smaller than pick-pocket's, and
Bigger than they cut their moustache with
Or the sweets called ludos cooked -
In the milk-fat of yellow cows -
They hail him, - and her's, thoroughfed -
But he tramples on their knees
Having comeout from scheming
All charging slants of blames -
Spitting on lies, - he defends what?
Borrowed and bought slogans
'give them a piece of bread'
They are your unpaid servants
Rights are little charities -
Dignity is just giving them enough
Of the old clothes too long too short
'they must look dirty and absurd'
These servants and little creature -
This unconscious mass of humans,
After holy recitation and anthem
They raise their hands -
For his long life and his thieving ways.

Dr Sadiqullah Khan's themes are social, spiritual, and politically aware. Delving deep into sufferings and joys, he seems to be a voice of the dispossessed, of the poor with whom he passionately identifies. He belongs to Wana, South Waziristan in Pakistan.

Poems by TemitopeAina

Scarred

The heat scorched tender skin burnt
Scarred beyond recognition who would have thought
This element could hurt and char what was once tender
What anguish and pain beyond description
Fire burnt me but loving hands healed me
The bandages like ghosts still haunt me
Why deceive please relieve me
The stigma deepens in to the soul
The jagged lines molded into my skin
Oil soothes balm caresses
The desperation is extremely soul deadening
Road to recovery and ensuing therapy
Leads me to your hospice
Your kind smile renews
Pray whilst I open up give me healing for these sores
The fire is doused but my heart hurts
It could never be like before as the needles

Whispers to the Broken Heart

Calm your broken heart
Favored one
Why weep at dawn and through the night
Why wall yourself in and mourn
Truly you loved and now you hurt
your lover went his way
His love so poignant so excruciating
yet you have seen another day
Beloved, lovers come and go
Love yourself even more
give yourself the chance to grow
like a seed buried in the soil
The memories make you cry
they are a lesson in disguise
the time has come yes this is the year
to prune your wings and fly
Maturing comes with pain
you have fully come of age
you need support and those whose love
can tenderly show the way
A man loves but human he is
you are the spiritual anchoring
so stop giving where unappreciated
and resist begging to be uplifted
You have survived so many storms
Now he carried the roof away with his hurt
Let the rain pour in and wash away
The sham collection he called love

Love yourself dear mine first
Cry but open your eyes even more
Life is a journey not a race
There are many companions along the way.

TemitopeAina is a renowned Nigeria Poet and fast-rising writer.

Poems by Jabulani Mzinyathi

Honourable

Do I detect some irony here
When they call you honourable
When you are bereft of honour
When dishonor is your hallmark
That word mangled beyond recognition
The foul stench of dishonour everywhere
There in your fast imported cars
When the roads are pock marked
Like the victims of small pox
When you own multiple farms
While the landless are still the homeless
When they till the now tired, arid land
Where is the honor honorable sir, madam
When all you clamor for are diplomatic passports
To hide behind diplomatic immunity grabbing and stealing
To hide in diplomatic bags the stolen diamonds
While the people of Chiadzwa wallow in poverty
When billions of dollars vanish like dew in the morning
Tell me honorable where is your honor
When this dissenting voice you brutally crush
With plastic bullets, water cannons, chocking tear smoke
When the baton does its dance of death on my soul
And when all you do is wantonly destroy flora and fauna
Do I detect some irony here honourable sir, madam

Jabulani Mzinyathi is a Zimbabwean to the marrow, and a firm believer in the Peter Tosh philosophy that there will be no peace if there is no justice. Jabulani is a pan-African and a world citizen.

Poems by Nungari Kabutu Wilfred

Black and Free

Freedom is no fear

If I could only have half that

To have a voice

To have my hands steady

To have my voice smooth

To be a black woman, free

An ugly black woman, beautiful in many ways.

To feel great and bold

To dance without watching my back

To walk and my steps be heard

To be a black woman, free

An ugly black woman, beautiful and strong

The pale think me ugly

But am an ugly beautiful woman

Fighting to be heard

Fighting to receive affection.

Fighting for respect

a beautiful black woman fighting for her children

a beautiful black woman

Bold Face to Freedom

Hers is a dark tunnel,
One I wish not to trend,
Where hope does not trend
She's overwhelmed and depressed
what she faces is unchangeable it seems
Trapped in a bleak situation
with no hope for rebirth or resolve
her back bears the memories of pain
Inflicted by the one who earthed her
Her father one of her mother's loyal clienteles
probably one with the insatiable desire for younger blood
She has lost her innocence to no prince charming in her secret childhood fantasies
Contrary to parents nature of protection
Her mother is the source of her emotional roller coaster
The marks on her hands bear witness,
the dig-ups done by the hands of a witch
Society grown cold to the cries of the unfortunate,
Abandoned too by the justice system that is potbellied from hefty bribes
She has learnt to lull herself to sleep with the stinging pain from her loins and back.
Today marks the end of it all she hopes,
For today she has made up her mind,
To have no one violate her to enrich the ungrateful witch
The price of her liberation a massive one to pay,
The once beautiful Natalie has no face but a mask
Her new face of liberation, the burns on her face inflicted upon her, from the steaming illicit liquor Now the deaf and blind world listens and sees, her bold, wrinkled face to freedom Crowned at last she feels.
In cuffs the witch exits.

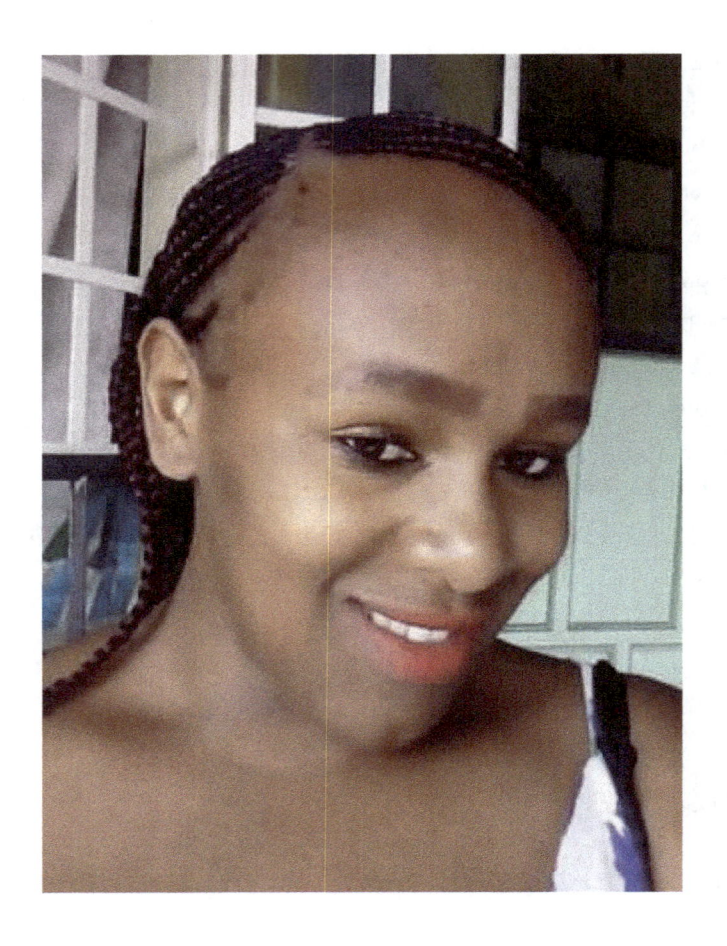

Nungari Kabutu Wilfred is a Kenyan poet, academic, and advocate of social justice.

Poems by Khadijah Finesse

No Mercy

She was an orphan
both parents gone
her name when translated meant mercy
But when she was scorned, sworn
or violently beaten. No sign of mercy
was she shown.
A beautiful young mother
of three was she.
Her curves still amazingly firm
of birthing two beautiful girls and
a bonny boy all under the age of nine
her body showed no sign.
Still grieving the untimely death
of her second husband
Young widow of twenty-seven that she was
barely a year since his death. She fell
for the charms of a man she thought
would fill the void her late husband had left.
Thought he'd give her
the love and care she craved and missed
Lonely for the warm comforting arms of security. The feeling of being desired
the taste of being kissed.
Loneliness for affection
blinded her to his aggression
His lies, cheating, jealous rages
the ultimate lack of respect

Manifest through violence.
Demoralized, beaten down and ashamed
He planted the seed of low self-esteem
deep within her being. So she accepted
His make-up kisses, after being beaten
Black and blue. Strangely and sadly looking upon the bruises and marks
as proof of loves existence.
Ignoring numerous voices of reason
Voiced by by concerned friends, neighbours
Onlookers even passersby.
All dire warnings and advice fell on deaf ears
Returning all with a smile so jaded
Yet beautiful still. Self esteem so low
Reduced to shreds by constant abuse
She appeared to just not care.
Eventually when she came up
As from one drowning. Reaching up
From under all the abuse.
Unfortunately it was too late.
For in the throes of merciless physical abuse
She succumbed to her wounds.
She'd been beaten to death.
Aged just twenty-seven
When in his alchoholic haze
Realising she was dead her abuser fled

Khadijah Finesse is a poet, GirlChild activist and perfoming artist from Zimbabwe.

Poems by Bina Sarkar Ellias

Syrian Nightmares in Kansas City

Thought it was a tank
rolling down the street
but it wasn't.
It was leaves rustling
in the wild wind.
Thought it was a gun shot
in the street below
but it wasn't.
It was a gaping gate
shut by the wild wind.
Thought it was a scream
in the neighborhood
but it wasn't.
It was a piercing whistle
of the wild wind.
Thought it was the wild wind
hissing past my door
but it wasn't.
It was an Israeli missile
claiming my blood, and more.

Bina Sarkar Ellias is a poet, fiction writer, and art curator from India. She is also founder-editor-designer-publisher of International Gallerie, the award-winning global arts and ideas journal.

Poems by Mohammed C. Jalloh

When I Was a Slave

From night in day
And twilight in dawn
A sound rings in my ear
Of slavery dinner
That scrub me drafting
the comfort of my next home
In ship of canoes
I was never good
In bleeding the pus
Of my jungle skin
Like kunta kinty
In the air of the ground
I was brought the life of torment
That curse the spirit of judgement
In secure mess that led to my suffering room
Of beautiful sore in slavery
In my body was the beating of drum
That entertains the lives
Of Portuguese master
And the soul of American masters
That makes the European nobles
Flip the hair of their happy daughters..
The triangle of slavery
Was the meat to my gut
Rice to my saliva

In the cost of shocking salad
That bath and choked me in hunger
I was the life of kunta kinty
That ran in imbuktu
For the ownership of my land
To flow in the memory of my brain
And the remembrance of my heart
For the place of my ancestors
Is in the mind of my skull
Even in the boat of their slaves
And the plane of their disheartenment..
Instead of bathing with soap
and water,
I was forcefully scrubbed
with sand and wring with mud
Indeed I envisaged freedom for the talent of my dance amused their children In the midst of guiltiness
For the cost of my godly gifts
was the only happiness to their joy
That makes their food tasteless in their tongues..
Dancing kitikata katakiti
I was used to entertained
their children
With my ancestry dance
from Timbuktu..
And so I smell the stars
of emancipation
In the seven ground of my
Dreamless ribs that shows
Me the real dream at last..

Lost Syria

gun rushes and sleeps
Beside Syrians windows
In pillow form
exploded midnight
And hit the Line of crisis
That
jumps in to slippery conflict
Kpao! Kpao!
Was the only sound hear
in breeze
Of Footprints wonder
As the greeny fund
Of guns distract the
Cities of beautiful Syria
From Damascus to Ghoutta
The dust and sand
Rise in disaster to swim
Children in blood
and
Crust women
in cemetery
Freedom lie
in Flood
And hatred rise
in peace
As love falls like snow
A beautiful city
Is now the city
Of burning crisis

Oh God
I weep in tears
Oh Allah
I bow in shame
In prayer I prostrate
and say,
Oh Allah
Free Syria
to everlasting peace
And passionate love
For its melodious name
the world praised
is now the bloody headlines
of creeping medias

Mohammed C. Jalloh is an academician, writer, and children's rights advocate. He's a Liberian by nationality, studying public administration and sociology at the African Methodist Episcopal University (AMEU) in Monrovia.

Poems by Nancy Ndeke

Fired

By a flame distantly close,
Doubt consumed by prose,
From a well bubbling in faith,
Of a dream long held in breath,
No day is like another,
Though sameness is the theme,
Matters of the heart it's cream,
Hold court in high strung seconds,
A race of time in stoppage of records,
The calendar looks on bemuse,
As the clock locks on the muse,
A high note of poesy divine,
A land opens it's gates fine,
Home is more than the castle high,
House is special abode right,
Such is the tale of doves of love,
Pecking cheeks on the highways of life,
Silence in tears of dizzy spell,
Magical in it's tone of tell,
For dew speaks of a dimming night,
And too a whetting of an appetite right,
Who sings but he who is happy,
Who whistles but he who secretly knows joy,
The rain is known to ride on a cloud,
Not so love in the crowd,
But in couplets of time spent,
The debt of love in emotion's pent,

Such is the applause of final call,
When the sun in it's glory fall,
At the supplicants knee,
Thanking deity for bringing hope in feel,
That which completes the circuit of pangs long in wait,
Love is a river,
Lovers are the drops,
That the entire river twirl in dance,
As two becomes one,
Undiluted,
Undaunted,
Unafraid,
For difference is assumption,
And same is accession,
To height's only the unafraid dare.

I Speak

For the burning bush and running deer,
Those that know no rest from a creature dull,
He wrecks life just because,
His sport bleeding shot's just because,
I speak streams of fearsome tears,
For the jumbo wild unsafe,
The rhino with its calf unsafe,
The wailing teak plucked for fun,
By a creature spoiling for a fight,
Stretching his muscular rifle for a shot,
Felling life just because,
I stammer at the wantonness open,
Clearing bushes for commercial bus,
Unfeeling tractors thundering at water sheds,
Scattering paupers out with thirsty throats,
A season too late, parched throats crack with death,
I shudder with ethos at the drilling roles,
Of multinationals secular rapes,
Open ulcers left to ferment among the displaced,
They howl to the moon with empty bowls,
Crude merchants feeding their crooked looting,
Leaving owners, ownerless,
I rest not at ease at all,
My soul protests,
My heart beats oddity,
To hear the silence on the lips of celebrants,
Toasting wine and stolen kisses,
On a cruise ship in the open seas,
Retelling lies of sumptuous meals grabbed from shrunken bodies of men ashore,

Where body count piles by shovel daily,
And human carcasses litter the plains of pain,
As corporeal looters fly aloft with the ease of a kite,
I tremble with rage at rape celebrated,
I gnash my broken teeth from the injustice visited,
Upon children,
Whose fault,
Remain birth in Africa,
And other spots where interests lay,
I pray,
Soundless tearful prayers,
And shame of my curse comes out loud,
That the heart that plans evil,
Should die not,
Before tasting the cup of sorrow,
That others so generously poured,
It's not revenge, it's not hate,
It's only a fair feel of how the shoeless feel,
Running for dear life,
While you keep truck on your cross hair of your powerful gun.

Billed But Still Barred

As entries and exits go, uniformity informs,
Come in between and chambers divide,
For one is location and the tendencies of his terms,
For another, it's shades and hues of his eyes,
And push germinates racing to shove,
Aligning lies with texts glittering,
As to why them and us must stay the divide,
Scheme's abide in plenty,
If it's not gods it's lesser genes,
If it's not class, it's lower brains,
To spread and root agragarious biases to toe blind eyes,
Culminating not just in flagged pride,
But wholesale tyranny often gravious.
While truth lags under pseudo intellectual creditors,
Those, who benefit in trillions,
At ill gotten gains from planted uprisings,
At times, the same saviors coming for help,
With quarters and dimes for show,
To give to one who give via esteemed robbery.
The tragedy of trading systems that rules the free world.

Nancy Ndeke is a widely published, multi-genre writer from Kenya. She writes poetry, hybrid essays, reviews, commentary, and memoir.

Poems by Milimo Chinimbwa

Rhythm of Distress

It's a furnace of distress
Boiling at the highest point
Melanin burnt off epidermis
Yet we are loft by many
Close mates now keep clear
Even family is not near
Just as a plant dries or withers
So do the hopes varnish in vain
Blaring the aspirations of gain
Determination burnt to ashes
Dedication damaged by heat waves
Elimination the rhythm of distress
A soul neglected by most folks
A life declared by many as moribund
A song sang with a rhythm of distress
Skin color covered by red patches
Superficial skin layers roasted to first degree
Swelling pain, redness and blistering dermis
First to firth degree burns giving birth to discrimination
Heat, cold, friction, the agents of the rhythm of distress
Radiation, hate, jealous, elements of the rhythm of distress

Cracked Calabash

Cracked and bundled in a heap is my broken calabash
Vicious vampires vent their vengeance on my varnished calabash Properly poking my pot to proper pieces
Their rage still roars like a lion in a cage
Venting their bloody blows on my broken calabash
Their breath stinks like dog carcasses in open space
A sad song sang by special sad singers sounds around my calabash
But nothing that is evil last forever
The waves of the sea rises and falls every day
Just like an elevator goes up and comes down
The waves will flow and patch up the broken pieces of my calabash
Endurance is an assurance and forbearance is a virtue
My calabash will stay broken but not for long
The broken calabash will soon live and sing a new song!!!!

Milimo Chinimbwa is a radio personality, educator, arts projects administrator, writer, and poet from Zambia.

Poems by Daniel Amakor

Beauty Behind Scars

Once as beautiful as morning,
now victims of circumstances.
New deformed bodies from
Their mistakes or that of men ,
accidents that took them unawares,
And the wickedness of man
unleashed upon their innocent bodies.
Tears weren't enough,
the pains were no match,
their loud cry had no effect,
as their bodies took it all.
Abnormal shape they've got,
a new way of life to live.
Eyes that seeks for our love,
Soul that yearns for our care.
Angels before the burn,
angels within after,
Still with their big hearts
in that deformed body.
If you happen to come across one,
try looking beyond the figure standing,
For only then will you see
beauty behind the scars.

Constructive Criticism

No! no!! no!!!, not at all.
I've never been the same again.
Your showers of mock appraisal,
is pulling me deep down.
Sinking me in my ignorance,
leaving nothing strong enough to hold unto.
Letting me fall head down like a meteor,
with great force and extreme speed.
Claiming to be tough and strong,
I only cried in my heart to elude pity.
I knew I am withering in summer: unusual,
my leaves falling down though green.
I feel my main me wearing off,
calling forth the other me I've made.
So so full of myself,
playing deaf as knowledge calls,
Right now, I'm hanging loose on air,
swaying in all cardinal directions,
wailing for words that will pull me up again.
Heads aching for advice
Heart willing to be criticized.
Criticize me I plead,
Criticize me I beg of you.
Your words only can draw me up,
draw me up out of my aloofness.
Just few words,
only few constructive criticism will be okay.

Ambassador Daniel Amakor is a young Nigerian playwright, short story writer, actor and poet, engaged in professional writing since 2013. His subjects range from the ultramicroscopic things on earth to the most significant things around. Having written for tele-stages and journals, he was awarded a barge as an outstanding poet.

Poems by Tracey C Nicholson

What Lies Beneath

I wear shades but
I still feel your shadow.
Beneath my hat pulsates a mind
plagued with fear.
You have no clue
of the road I walk
yet you snigger and gawk.
These gnarled, charred knobs are the
feeding hands you had bitten.
My indigo blouse now shrouds
a dark musty place.
layered cosmetics and fancy brows
hide a ravaged, scarred face.
Your stares are like bullets
Your words like knives.
Sometimes I smile
while my nerve slowly dies.
You spit your poison because my countenance is strange -
I pretend I am deaf
at your vile and venomous vein
but your words pierce the heart
beneath my indigo shame.
And deeper still
pickles a soul torn apart -
The mind beneath the hat;

the face arched by fancy brows;
Beneath all these masks and scars
you will simply find,
a girl who has a dream to live her life free from words
that pierce the heart, beneath
her indigo blouse.

Tracey C Nicholson is an advocate of peace, and for burn survivors, and a human rights activist from South Africa.

Poems by Anu Soneye

Rhythms of War

I hear the gongs.
Ugo Ugo Ugo.
The rhythm of war.
The panting of warriors.
Far on the other side
I hear cries of children
and men, crouched with their wives
underneath tables and chairs.
I see fear, walking their land
and terror flashing in the eyes.
Who dare holds faith,
when the tip of a poisoned spear
Squeals out the heart of a brother
and what prayer is left,
when the axe-head digs through the
Skull of a sister?
I hate this rhythm
This metal music that feeds on souls.
I hate,
the burns,
the ruins of conflict,
the spring of bloodshed,
the field of dead men,
I hate,
the aftermath of war.

How Can We Breathe?

when our throats are held by the hands of oppression
or live,
when our nostrils,
blocked by mucus of corruption?
I do hear that there is light at the end of every tunnel.
But what then happens to me,
a black child,
with black blood,
birthed under poisoned skies
Poisoned skies that oozes the steam of darkness?
Aduke and Amoke,
my sisters.
Come,
Join me at the table.
Join me so that we can look each other in the face.
Let's make the table ready.
so that when hunger comes through the rumbling streets of our stomachs,
we can rub each others tummy.
Abayomi my brother!
How long are we going to use sleep to chase away thirst?
For how long are we going to watch our future seep away like a leaking fuel tank?
stop looking at me.
Speak to me before I invite mama's segi's devils to take me home.

Anu Soneye is a poet, writer, and artist from Nigeria.

Poems by Annette Swann

Burnt Face — Forgiven

In the blink of an eye you scarred me for life
Burnt Face was the taunt that cut like a knife
The trauma, suffering, pain and tears
How did you live with your guilt for all these years
Your absence and silence, I ask you to reflect
What path my life took due to your neglect
It took years of struggle to break down the mental bars
That forced me to focus so much on my physical scars
A mother's love and courage made me grow strong
She blamed herself for your actions for far too long
Dear lord I want to be normal in every way
Each night I prayed to god for the scars to go away
As a child I only saw today not how the future would look
As an adult I put my thoughts and memories into a book
Cathartic as it was, I grew to understand
It was all an accident and nothing was planned
If one day I get the chance to look you in the eyes
You will see me as a phoenix from the ashes I will rise
To offer you forgiveness for all that has been done
My life is full of love and joy and my journey has been won!

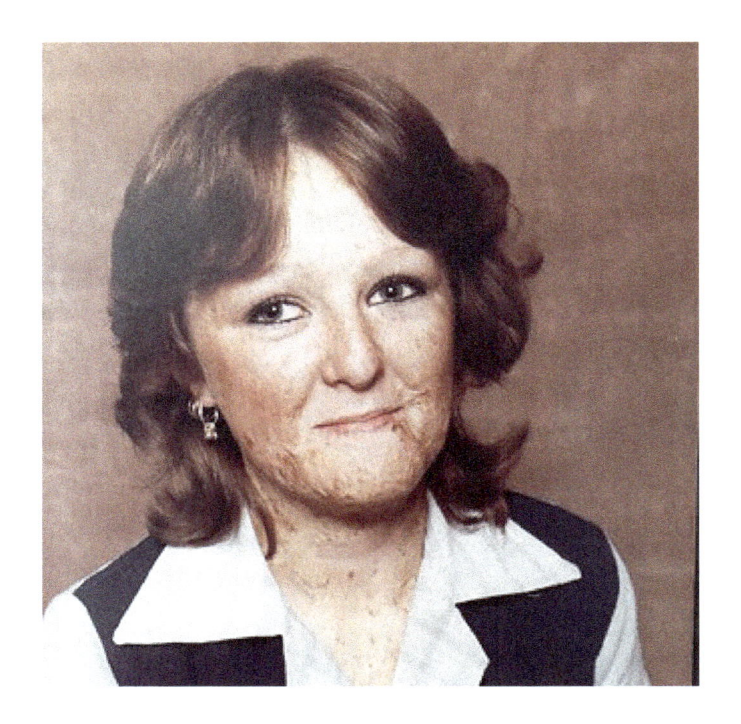

Annette Swann is an Australian author, freelance writer, editor, and burn survivor. She serves as a Goodwill Ambassador for the South African CAMPIO Burns Group and has a Bachelor of Arts Degree in Public Relations and Communications and a Diploma of Multimedia.

Poems by Caroline Adwar

Life Changes

The scars so real
Within and without
The blazing tongues eating at every soul that tried to rescue..
His cry of pain dying down with the seconds ticking.
Overwhelmed with the lashing and boring like the nails on our Lords hands and feet.
Tossing and turning at the thought
Years down the line...
A fire firing up, not a sight to behold.
The scars bear witness of the same
Who was once human
Only human as they walk
A nose gone
An eye gone
The skin that was so silky and smooth
Now a fold of burnt flesh
Ah! Beauty is a word for a time
Children running away in fright
Away from their mother..
All mirrors destroyed
For she cannot bear the reflection of who she has become
It eats into her very being...
All she wants, her children to accept her
It wasn't her fault...
She was at the right place...
At the wrong time..
At last...a reprieve!

The red cross had come to her aid
But the money....
She looked to the skies and cried!
The attendand watching keenly
Wondering how a human could be so faceless!
A picture she carried with her of the days when SHE WAS!
A far cry from what she had become
She gave her a listening ear
Saw her previous self...
Tried to maintain her calm..but a tear escaped from her eye...
She would help this woman retrieve her lost glory.......
The plastic surgery was a success!
But what about the thousands that did not get a guardian angel?
The mother of two walked away a happy beautiful mum...
Her children stealing glances at her,
Wondering if she was the one!

Caroline Adwar is a fast rising poetess, and an English and music teacher in Kenya. She started writing poetry while in high school and she is a fanatic of old English poetry writing, traditional style, rhyme, repetition, alliteration, and assonance. She is currently experimenting in African free verse and her poetry will soon be published in Kenya, Zimbabwe and other International platforms.

Poems by Paul Oladipo Kehinde

Express Myself

These walls can never incarcerate my parietal lobe or sensory cortex
These leg iron chains are a frailty and can't hostage my concentration
Yes they say prison has robbed my sanity and thus inanity because
I find vanity in manifesting the desires of my heart in these expressions
These iron bars are too small to suppress my meditation, you see comrades
The strong suit of my attention grasps every destination,
I mean my deep thoughts got me slaying in chains. You see
All these graffiti in the walls, all these drawings, painting, singing
And chanting you witness from this tank, are a reality of my imagination and
Enhanced interrogation techniques cannot suffocate my expression or
Demolish the exhibition of my imagination neither can any abuse
Abuse my expression because I still have to express the oppression
So on whatever condition, I still have every reason to believe I'm still
Living because after all I can enjoy the fantasies I have of my heart through expressing.
I have experienced all the mysterious jungles of my desires and you
all these walls around us comrades, live to tell the story my eyes long to see.
Chains don't ever block expressions here is a beautiful lady, enjoy cdes

Fly With Me

I will fly away with the wings of my mind
I will fly to the end of the sky
I will fly with the thoughts of victory
I will fly and fly with words
Strength for my growing heart
I will fly with eyes of vision
I will fly with thoughts of victory
There is magic in belief
just spread the wings of your mind
fly with me
away with songs of victory

Paul Oladipo Kehinde is a poet, writer, and literary arts activist in Nigeria.

Poems by Nwuguru Chidiebere Sullivan

Celebration of Indignation

Therein I go again to register my pains
Having forgotten how long I've spent in this servitude's den
Therein I go again shouting out my anguish
To the ears of yesterday and today
For they too, know how tears deserted my eyes
I think I died yesterday
I know it was not just today's oppression
Of course not
But the heaviness of 1967'S lost
Weighed me down till death
My heart is now rusted
For it no longer pump blood but rusts of pains
I no longer count my hope in primes
For all I know now is in odds---3,5,7...
While they plot more chaos for me 2 4 7
I no longer fear marginalization
For I've grown affinity for it;
These days, tunes of tribal bigotry
No longer worry me for I'm used to it;
It's being compelled to watch in dismay
How cattle raid my ban that kill the me in me
Aye, hope is a gem
but for how long will I wear marginalization
around my neck?
For sure, it's more than a century now

That I've worn these shackles of enslavement
on my waist
always hopping and hobbling with a hiss all day
like a caged bird.
I celebrates indignation with no hope
For I only translate my pains into ink-fall
With flows of salt less tears that is tasteless
Plugging on pains of countless mass burial
My eyes witnessed at Nimbo,Abia and Benue
This ought to be a Satire
But I retired my insinuation
When I noticed it's no poem nor fun
For it's obvious they transferred Gene of Marginality
From my grandfather to my father
Then to me and now they hope for my child.
Melancholy people don't talk much
Especially when their intestines are bonded with resentment
But I have to say this,
"Freedom! Freeeedom is all I cry for,
Get this shackles of suppression off me
Or risk seeing me go my way ".

Nwuguru Chidiebere Sullivan of Nigeria is a student of medical laboratory science in Enonyi State University.

Poems by Ibrahim Clouds

Africa — One of a Kind

Africa - one of a kind,
a black star- in a white sky.
A distinct pearl- amidst white corals,
we are the bell- ringing good morals.
Africa fine women- with adoring tribal marks-
their smiles mean good omen- their laughter show the fair gap-
between their frontal snow-like white teeth,
and when they dance- they control drum beat,
with each steps as if controling the wind-
their waist beads, as they dance, exclaim "africa! Africa! Africa". They are
the goddess of the kitchen-
eat their food, forget the date of your naming ceremony.
They are the sweet mermaid of the bed;
every night is heaven for Africa men.
Africa men- one of a kind,
brave- strong men- not scared of war,
with bare hands- they kill hyenas,
and their voice spans the world for a tour.
Africa men with skull of wisdom,
without a sword, they win kingdoms.
Well-secured are the African women in their arms,
against the eagle- they protect Africa with their arms.
Africa children- one of a kind,
climbing the neck of mountains
at their very tender age,
picking sluggish silly snails-
after every meteor rain,

from the dark hearts of forests-
where wet leaves shed silent tears.
Africa children are one of a kind-
to heaven; they send their kites through the sky.
Africa- One of a kind-
a distinct black star
in the white spreading sky.

Is Halloween in Bangladesh

Is it Halloween or what?
For the faces covered with masks.
Can I get one for my cuzz?
He likes Halloween and fine masks.
Twas a baptism of acid!
alas! baptism of acid.
Bangledesh- baptised with this water,
that rapes the face of beauty's tower.
Ah! that satanic water!
that eats the eyes and the skull!,
it leaks the brain like butter,
it eats the flesh to the core.
Stop! stop that baptism!
of a satanism.
Stop the burning of flesh!
stop the roasting of teeth.
stop the boiling of breast!
stop the baking of ribs.
Stop defacing Bangladesh!
stop burning her fine skirt.

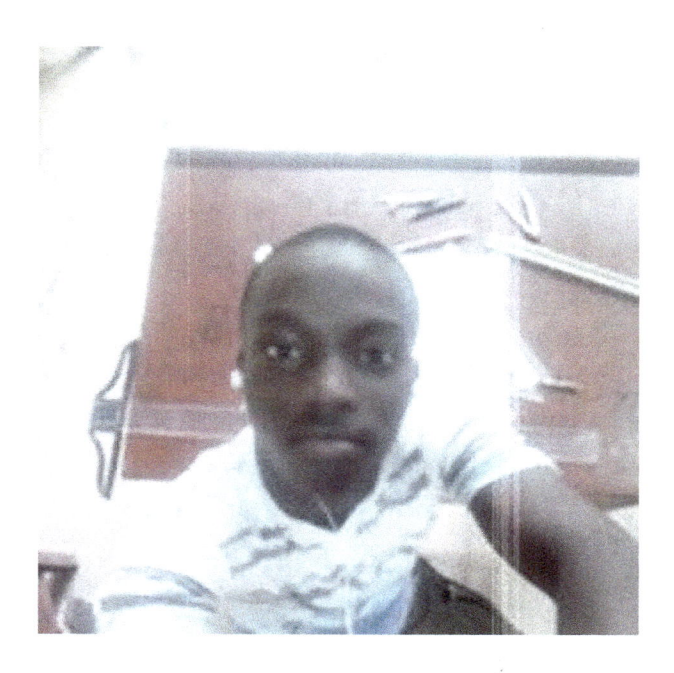

Ibrahim Clouds is a Nigerian poet. He spend 90% of his time in seclusion, meditating, reading spiritual books, and writing. He studied science for three years in Wesley College of Science Elekuro Ibadan Nigeria. He is currently studying architecture in the Polytechnic Ibadan Nigeria.

Poems by Opeyemi Joe

The Oligarchs

Do not be taken in by their egrets' snowy wings
Or be inveigled by their phalanx format in flight,
Do not be enchanted by their long, landly legs stealthy
Amongst the sleeping golden grasses
Or be deceived by their yellow pelicaned mouths
Or spelled be by the curvy grace of their swanned necks…
Follow the spoors of their treads and you will find them at banquets
Dining with Devil himself, with lengthy silvery spoons
Scooping mouthfuls of maggots into their guts
Squirming maggots from the spread on their host's table;
Follow their lead and you will see their
Angelic companies in the city's madden
Seeking out friendlies, those living off the dumped, rotting dead
Squabbling amongst themselves over the hulk of a carcass
The humongous corpse of Chinua Achebe's country.

Opeyemi Joe writes from Ibadan, Nigeria. He has had his works featured in journals, reviews, and anthologies the world over. He likes soccer and singing, in that order. He is also a geologist.

Poems by Tracy Yvonne Breazile

Osmithila

Tin shed shack houses lined the barren sands
Little dirt floor houses on barefoot trail.
Took that knife and slit my hands
Distressed indifferent encampment tale
Check in only to retire
Stoke the fire.
Been here so long, I lost time
Departed nomad's plumes of smoke rise
And merge into the leaden sky
Contemplated walked for weeks
Haunting wretched mess.
Poke the fire.
Beach of Bones over that way
Labyrinth down the way just past the mine
South African sun will burn you alive
Cast horrid plumes of dust.
They never come back.
Stoke the fire.

Zimbabwean Voices

That stolen flame of the voices cryin' freedom
Causin' shattered voices
With clouds of chaos pretending purpose
And false doctrines dictate
Shallow hopes that embrace
Talk of freedom and feelin' secure
In the shadows linger shards of hauntin' security
Folks with two faces and false freedoms
Cryin' loud from maddened minds and maddened voices

And an impasse point of purpose
Sling slogans of false secure dictates
And passing fancy lending false embrace
To the dreamers of wanderin' embraces
And holdin' hopes and huntin' security
Calling to the winds with their dreams of freedoms
And sing songs of dreaming voices
Of the greater good and aim the purpose
Toward the echoes of conscious dictates
Partner freedoms with reasonable dictates
Offer their brethren kind embraces
Sing new songs of solid security
And carry dreams of fairness and freedom
Cause to pen truths and sound their voices
And call them to the grand purpose

And find that common purpose
That sifts all the slinging dictates
And carry that kind embrace

With certain truths and certain security
In the melting pot of basic freedoms
And echo the dreams of their voices
And grant them their laughin' voices
With honest and powerful purpose
And hide the unfair dictates
With cool hearts that offer empty embraces
And shed the land of insecurity
And breed the dreams of fair freedoms
Dreamers with those freedom speaking voices
With power of purpose to dismiss cruel dictates
And all embrace signs of stability and security

Tracy Yvonne Breazile is a writer living in the United States of America. She was granted the opportunity to serve as Writer/Mentor in Residence with the 2018 Zimbabwe We Want Poetry Mentorship Program originated by Mbizo Chrirasha.

Poems by Awadifo Olga Kili

Tanga

Here is hunger famished starving Tanga
Her eyes blink with every ray of the frail sun
in her winter of want.
Clouds are not fertile,
Her belies echo with sorrow and emptiness
pulls away her breathe.
Tanga is dying under the watch of greying day
and scavenging birds
Waiting for benevolence from a Good Samaritan.

Her frame is hopeless and tired.
Her heart dances lazily to the merriment
fleas ready to devour her perishing self.
Worms and greenflies signal her demise
They eat and sup from her festering limp.

Tanga is famishing, starving under our watch
Tanga groans under the stone of sorrow.
Scythe of misery gyrate her mind to madness.
Tanga lost her education and future
Long back to cruel hunters.
Tanga lost her dreams to the haters
Tanga was offered as a child bride.
The fire in her eyes are long gone.
The dance in her heart is fading.

Awadifo Olga Kili is a Ugandan author, poetess, law student, and human rights activist. She is the author of the books *Victorious Tales* and *Echoes of Wails*. Kili represents young women and girls and is a Young Writer's Representative from Uganda in Womawords Hall of Fame, an international literary community that hosts female writers across the World. Some of her poems have been featured in journals and anthologies internationally.

Poems by Omwa Ombara

A Dirge of Hope to Sudan

Sudan the great has fallen
A million salty tears cannot fill the Nile
The land of giants has dwarfed into shadowy ghosts
Red eyes cannot light the cooking stones
Offended spirits roam the land in search of their former selves
Chaos reign, the scorching sun cooks animal carcasses
The calves have died with milk on the teats
Vultures long dead are not invited to the feast
The dead cannot bury the dead
Lord of tears, rescue me.
Death has camped in Sudan
The source of the River Nile has been defiled into a desert
The wicked Janjaweed beat death drums
The cobweb of impunity weaves corruption, greed, war
Foreign arms grind machinery of destruction
Endless power hunger games rip open wombs of pregnant mothers
Isn't Killer games, the enemy's gain?
I cry but my tears have no gain
Not until Sudan rises again.
I sob.
Sudan's jails are filthy layers of stifled innocent souls
Charged with imaginary crimes from the head of a deranged government
A decayed tooth whose loose system leaves toothless smelly mouths, caves
Till when, Mama? Till when?
Peace talks are the rugs on which berserk leaders wipe their bloody feet
Caked soles of feet in Bloody shoes soaked in rivers of blood
Bashir the wicked jigger has fed on the flesh of his people for eons

His fleecy naughty bedbug toy guns flash a weeping trail of destruction
Not even the highest court in the world can hold him
The ICC, the leaders' kalongolongo children's game
I cry.
Sudan's crisis is the cry of many rivers
Sudan's Sickler, harvests death like a bottomless pit
Sudan has become an open grave
Loose shooting canon, fire spitting snakes
Life mocker, get away from me
The Buzz of a million houseflies is your favourite song
What day of the week, were you born?
You are a shame to the universe
Your brother's death does not stop your sleeping pangs
Your children, what? Child soldiers.
The leaders of Sudan have no brothers or sisters
Only enemies.
I cry.
Sudan's poverty is the joy of the colonizer
The master reigns supreme
Our leaders have opened the granary to strangers
Their green colored forest clothes the death signature
Sudan's helpless tears only dry up the barren soil.
Sudan's fake eyelashes have fallen
Adults cry like children and there are no children to cry
Darfur exposes the raw jaundiced eye of horror and injustice
Africa, North, South, East, West
Lamentations. Lamentations. Lamentations.
Sudan crisis is the cry of rivers of blood and tears
Rivers that flow in red blood and mixes with rich oil
Discolored by wars of greed, gold and oil
Sudan crisis is the cry of deserts
Turned into quarries of hidden guns

Sparkling in deadly smiles
As government eats her children
Sudan crisis, the naked cry of the earth
Earth filled with limbless bodies, ashes
Earth cannot recognize her own and feeds them to the worms
The justice train is slow no matter how fully you oil it
Women of Sudan arise
Save your children from these monsters who occupy state houses
Hold your wombs and breasts, invoke the power within
The children you suckled and nurtured have turned against you
The children have slipped from the nest and become monsters
You cannot give up
You must not give up
Mothers of Sudan, arise and claim your space
You have suffered enough
The senseless leaders have declared Sudan an orphan
Daughters of Sudan arise and fight back
The battle is yours, my sisters
Our hopes lie in you
Poetry Nation, Arise
You are the last weapon left standing
To rescue our sister Nation
Sudan.
I cry.

In Honor of Press Freedom Day 2020

(Satire)

I am an armchair journalist scouting Zuckerberg's ever busy streets for free information
Feeding off the sweat of frontline journalists and eyewitnesses
Taking credit for those who risk their lives everyday in the COVID-19 war to bring the news home.
I am an armchair journalist, I work in pyjamas and bathroom slippers
I sip endless cups of coffee and hug my whiskey bottles against my protruding potbelly.
I am Media
Proclaiming freedom of speech to justify my waywardness
Scrounging for leftover news to analyze, interpret, criticize.
I steal pictures faster than they hit facebook
Downloading, cropping, filtering.
I switch my remote control 24/7 to keep up with the latest news channels
Give me forty winks and I'll do the trick, I sleep with the pen and notebook on my lap for tips and balance.
I am the yellow journalist
Conveniently starved from the appetite of quoting sources
Too entitled to attribute websites and pages I have stolen from.
I am an armchair journalist
I celebrate press freedom today
Can't you see my armchair is rugged from my tired butt?
I am the press,
I hold the power of the pen.
I 'kill'people with rumors and post their photos before they truly die.
I do not use the share button
'Copy paste' and 'stolen'is my Press Plagiarism Card
I am an armchair journalist begging politicians and fans for donations to buy bundles and pay for internet.
I have not been to any COVID-19 spotlight zone

I'm so afraid to die
And leave all the news behind
Let the other journalists with spine sweat it out in the hot seat.
I am the armchair journalist
Mocking journalists in jail, those murdered for speaking truth to power and asylees
Holding my large nose high in contempt
But I have thousands of likes and followers and I must feed my fans.
Don't you know 'image is everything'?
@authoromwaombara

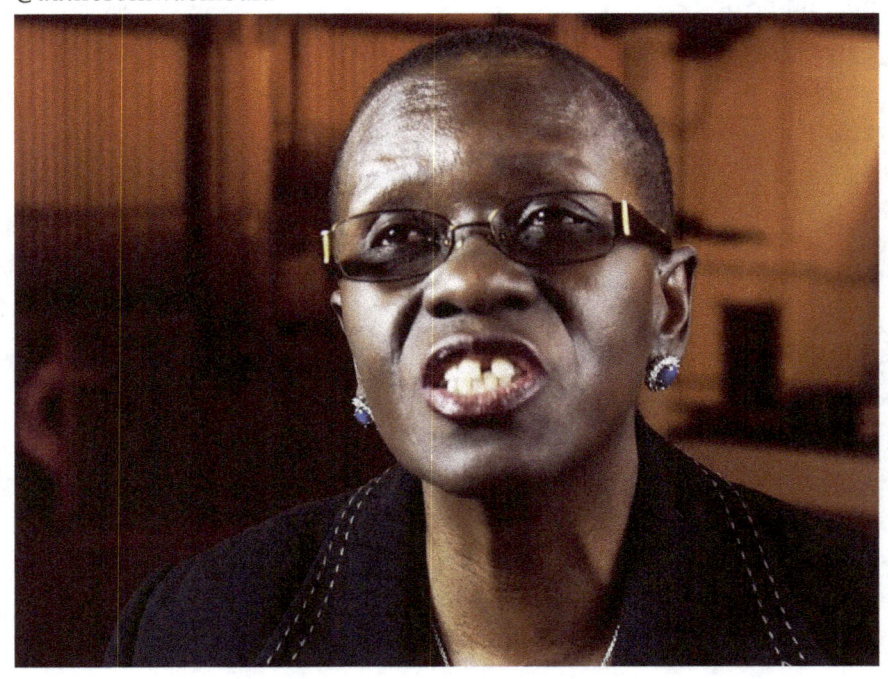

Omwa Ombara of Kenya is a prolific African voice in diaspora. Her resilience-hardened verses send a rebellious jab to the cantankerous, unrepentant COVID 19 pandemic. She sings a bitter hymn against chair warmers and lazy hands-on-keyboard scribes, who thrive on abusing and harvesting the sweat of resilient writers and voices from a digital thicket, without any ounce of their own effort.

Poems by Samuella J. Conteh

Beautiful Scars

Daring out from behind the shadows
She shakes off shackles of regrets
Draining her off herself.
Rummaging in the shambles
Of her yesterday,
She finds in her bruised being
A rare, priceless gem
Lying in a muddied state.
Venturing forth with determined vigour,
She pays a tear sacrifice
At the altar of the passing dawn.
Daring to stare into the gaze
Of a faceless tomorrow,
She marches into waiting hands
Gloved by grace .
She is a survivor with beautiful scars,
Smoothened out by the mercy
Of time and hope.

Hours in Reverse

My people are a resilient lot, with coping skills to match
Their jocular acumen can make dark days shades lighter
As they churn out sweet mirth from sordid situations
So I send up three cheers of hurray to my compatriots
Who would not crawl into corners of fear and hopelessness
Late into the night, I caressed my quill into a constant spill
Sweetly exchanging silent whispers with my abiding muse
My ears flapped wider to the sounds of dice thrown on glass
I smiled at the back of my neighbours chilling on a game of ludo
Days in lockdown would be long, so we spend them long into nights
As I scribbled, they threw their dice followed by laughter
Late into the night to the wee hours of lockdown day two
Me and my compatriots reversed hours to massacre boredom
I succumbed to sleep, to wake up still to their game of ludo
I was still cajoling my muse when their silence greeted the morn

Samuella J. Conteh is from Sierra Leone, West Africa. She is a writer, poet, dramatist, and motivational speaker. She is a member of the Sierra Leone Writers Forum and Member of the Board of PEN-SL. She is President of the International African Writers Association in Sierra Leone. Samuella's poems and short stories have been featured in several national and international anthologies. She has also received many awards including the Medal of Ambassador de Literature (ADL), Award of World Poetic Star, Award of Mahatma Medal, and the Order Of Shakes.

Poems by Michael (Dickel) Dekel

Nothing Remembers

where in our times we these rocks piled into buildings
that fell down a thousand years ago dis(re)membered from war
or earthquake raised and razed again into where nothing
recalls again the warm day anemones bloom hollyhocks
poppies forget no one and another rain day another dry day
pass hot and cold while an orvani drops blue feathers in flight
a hawk sits calmly on a fencepost and flocks of egrets
traipse toward the sea no cattle no grains all harvested
in this place we would call holy land nothing left to it but conflict
with the passing of her life that tried so hard to hang onto one
moment many moments missed so many more empty echoes
a difficult way to say goodbye to a mother watching her
evaporate like rain in the desert her mind dust that dries
lips her droned words faded as warmth from a midnight rock
meaning what the layers of history these rocks un-piled
reveal sepia photos a couple of tin-types dust school
reports cards newspaper holes the shells of bugs raised and razed
again and again into our times where nothing remembers

Michael (Dickel) Dekel, from Israel, has authored six published books and chapbooks (pamphlets) of poetry and short fiction, and published over 200 individually published poems, short stories, and non-fiction pieces, in addition to book reviews and academic articles. He has taught writing, literature, and English language in higher education in both the U.S. and Israel. Michael publishes an online blog-Zine (https://MichaelDickel.info/). He is the past chair of the Israel Association of Writers in English.

Poems by Jerusha Kananu Marete

Smile Again Katrina

Happy was she before the news,
Laughed her heart out before her woes;
She tumbled and tossed
With her son while they played;
When will Katrina smile again?

How could such news pass her by?
She hadn't gotten a wind,
She had been playing with her lad,
The breaking news broke her;
When will Katrina smile again?

There had been a serious attack,
In the camp where Kibby worked;
Many soldiers were feared dead,
When will Katrina smile again?

She checked the list,
Her eyes misty;
He was among the dead,
Her Kibby
When will Katrina smile again?

She broke down,
She wanted to die.

Her son thought it was a lie,
On the floor she sobbed
When will Katrina smile again?

She grieved mourning her sun,
And forgot her son;
She locked herself in her room,
Her life was now gloom.
Her all soaked in tears
When will you smile again Katrina?

Her son sank into depression,
Tried to get his mother's attention;
Katrina never got out of her room,
Your son needs you Katrina
When will you smile again?

During the burial
Her eyes sunk deep into the sockets;
Her mind far away,
Her face a blank stare,
A zombie:
When will Katrina smile again?

She went back to her room,
Broke glasses and whisky bottles
Fighting inner battles—
She was slowly losing her son;
Smile to your son, Katrina.

Sam sat silently in a corner doodling,
His room messy,

He didn't talk to anybody,
Hot tears scalding his cheeks.
Sam needed Katrina

She was about to do the worst:
She served whisky,
a cocktail with poison—
She was tired—
Your son is knocking, Katrina!

She looked at the glass;
She cried.
"Open the door, Mum;
I want to sleep next to you.
Why do you hate me, Mum?"
He was sobbing.
Come back to your senses, Katrina.

She went to open the door:
Her son was there, his nose bleeding,
She hadn't known, he was sick.
It was not time to cry, her son needed her.
I'm sorry, Katrina, take heart.

She gave her son first aid, but she was scared,
"I'm sorry, son," she told him.
Sam picked the poisoned glass,
He thought it was soda;
Katrina had forgotten about it—
She hit the glass off his hands.
You almost killed your son, Katrina.

Her son was shocked,
Mum had never been like that before.
Katrina lay on the floor, crying:
Stand up, Katrina; your son needs you.

Sam knelt beside her,
'Get up, Mommy,
I am here,
All will be well."
It's okay, Katrina; put yourself together.

She looked at her son,
She tickled him, he tickled her back and they fancied the tickles
and smiles for the first time in a long time;
She stood up,
Wrapped her son in a lingering hug:
"Come here little Kibby
We will get through this together."
She whispered
Sam imitated his late father:
"You look beautiful, Mrs Kibby.
Kibby misses you
But I love you more."
Katrina is laughing again.

Mau Mau Veteran's Wail

Why are you so heartless?
Why did God create a being so insensitive?
Why why why?

You ate my meat, you sucked my blood
And now you are refusing with my bone!?

We shared the tears, we shared a master
We shared the pain, went through hell together
I used my teeth to unchain you
Tore my tattered coat to cover your bleeding wounds
I silently wept when the master lynched you?
I confronted the master when he imprisoned you?
My courage made me lose my eye, I am partially blind
I did it for my brother!

In the bush we had sleepless night
You became our eye as we fought for our land
We waged battle in the forest, we fought in the mountains
We fought in red rivers, the white master gave up
He run to his white gardens, left our black heavens

Excitedly, we sang freedom songs
We almost kissed freedom, solidarity was our intention
We needed our own, not a master but a servant

We looked around, almost everyone had a dent
One had lost a leg, another had lost his teeth,
The other lost both legs, I had lost my eye

Protecting you from murderous master
You hadn't lost anything, you were fighting from the house
You also knew how to hide when we went for battles
They chained you and fed you from the forest we still protected you

We now needed our own who had no dent
Tumbo has no dent he became our leader
He knew how to write he became our leader

I vividly remember the day we crowned you our leader
I tried to talk to you but your mind seemed far away
Your lips were curved in a sinister smile eyes piercing through the sky
You seemed like a small god, immortal, you didn't see us anymore
I was worried for the first time, we became invisible
We disappeared into the tumult they were ranting your name
Fighting among themselves for coins the new master threw at them
Your soldiers were similar to soldiers of the former master
But their color was black!
We had hope when we waited!
We had hope when we fought!

You have eaten my meat, sucked my blood
Why are you refusing with my bone?
The bone is my graveyard, why are you grabbing my graveyard?
You want me to be buried in the air or to be devoured by vultures?

My children and grandchildren roam in the street
Others slaves in your estates
While you enjoy the freedom we fought for
I am old and eager to die, memories of my sacrifice kill me softly
But when i die, where will i be buried?
You have grabbed my meat, sucked blood

Why are you refusing with my bone?
My bone, my graveyard
Is it yet independence?

Jerusha Kananu Marete is a Kenyan writer, author of an anthology of poems titled *Echoes of Military Souls*. She has her heart in narrative poems. She graduated from the University of Nairobi with a degree in Education (English &Literature) and is currently an MA student at Kenyatta University (Literature/Theatre departments). Her poems have been published in Best New African Poets 2019 anthology.

Poems by Lingiwe Patience Gumbo

Still Here

The eyes shimmer in the sun's rays
The same which stared deeply into the soul
Diving into the inner most parts
Bringing peace, joy and love

The smile generating the Mexican wave
Just a moment for an embrace
A Hello, a good to see you again
Now the very thoughts of them
Keep their memory alive

Daily the heart's mind denies
"It is not possible, they are just around the corner"
The silliest gesture reminds us of them
That song, that scent which lingers long after
Their smile still lights up our world

Our minds are certain of the realities
Our hearts bleeding trying to make head to tale
Our eyes still see the gorgeous face, the dimples
A simple chill signals the mind to reach for the sweater, to keep them warm

Anniversaries, birthdays
Colors, flowers
The park, the pool

They flood our imagination
Each moment shared,
Still the flames burn bright

Only the flesh is absent
Only our touch can't be felt
But all the emotions have their usual dwelling
The heart still blushes when their name is spoken
Because they are still here

Time will heal all wounds
Not a time prescribed by someone
Nor one to stop the process of grieving
Yet the heart conditions the time spent
Time is all we need
Because they are still here.

To My Unborn Child Lingiwe

I am glad you are mine
I am also afraid I am yours
A mix of bitter sweet are my emotions
They engulf me as I think of you
Many are my hopes
Outside this your present abode
Many are the realities
You are bound to meet face to face

I know you are getting ready
Anxious of what lies out here
I too await your arrival
When I shall hold you in my arms
Giving thanks to the One
Who wove you together in the depths of my womb

I must school you of this world
That will soon be your dwelling place
Of the love that awaits you
From the one chosen for you by the Maker
The one who will show you the meaning of true love
The one person your heart will yearn for always

But, where love is hate also fights to belong
To cause havoc and discord
To take away the joy and peace and such treasures
It will come, not in form of a dragon with spikey horns
But with a smile, a laughter, a kiss, an embrace

Beware
Be tactful
Be wise
Even as you seek much counsel from your Maker
Lest you stumble and fall
As is their core calling for your life

Inspite of the corrupt minds
The harsh conditions
The times of lack in times of abundance
The times of pain and bleeding;
Your heart must understand
How it too must feel for others

Also remember you will find friends
Who will become your family
They will be all you need
And listen when you seek counsel
Our Maker will send his angels in our own flesh
To guide you through this journey of life
And help you keep strong
When the journey proves too long

Listen to your heart and care more
Love more, have mercy more
Reach out more, give more
Speak the truth clearly, be faithful, be all you can be
Learn more, try more
Because in others will you learn
To become great and useful

I wish to live with you
Every step of the way
But man's punishment awaits us all
It could be now
It could be after
But in all I wish you know
Of what is to come after
Because it will surely come
And so being prepared you must

As I impart this truth
From my heart to yours
From my soul to yours
May these words find a dwelling
A fertile soil
That it bears much fruit
That you also may pass on
To your unborn child

Lingiwe Patience Gumbo of Zimbabwe is an administrator and secretary by profession and a church volunteer teacher/advisor for adolescents. Gumbo is a singer-songwriter with an 8-track album titled "Worthy of All My Praise." Gumbo's poems are featured in various online platforms like miombopublishing and girlchildcreativity. She is the host of an online TV show, "NY Television," where she presents motivational messages on the Breakfast Nuggets, Tuesdays and Thursdays.

Poems by Beatrice Othieno-Ahere

From Chaos to New Order

In the midst of all the chaos
How do we bring back the harmony
How do we connect the disconnection
How do we get back our power, our will as one people
In the midst of the chaos
How do we sew back the 47 torn pieces
How do we unite in justice for all of us, make it our shield and defender
How do we account for the lives lost, never to be seen again, some disappeared, vanished, bodies hurt and maimed
In the midst of the chaos
How do we get back to building our nation, we need our jobs, put food on our tables, take care of us and our families, spare something for our brothers and sisters with less
In the midst of the chaos
How do we make religion work for us, not taken over by politics but a place of refuge that does not discriminate, does not take sides but unifies
In the midst of the chaos
How do we get back Kenya, how do we rid ourselves of divisive politics
How do we put the interests of the citizens first, how do we do this?
In the midst of the chaos
How do we get a rebirth, unlock our minds, usher in a new Kenya
In the midst of the chaos
How do we make the first step?
Is it possible for us, as Kenyans to re-elect new leaders who have us all at heart and stop the passing down of leadership as a family right but an

earned position
In the midst of the chaos
Yes it is possible to usher in a new Kenya
Yes, we can rebuild, rewrite, reboot, repost, retweet and pray for a positive narrative
In the midst of the chaos
There can be a new Kenya
From chaos to a new order

Beatrice Othieno-Ahere of Kenya is a creative spirit, with a deep and quiet soul. She has great belief in the motherland Africa and her richness often mistaken for poverty. Her passion is working with young people and women to amplify their powerful voices to maximize their potentials and break the chains that hold us back.

Poems by Jamie Dedes

One Lifetime After Another

one day, you'll see, i'll come back to hobnob
with ravens, to fly with the crows at the moment
of apple blossoms and the scent of magnolia ~
look for me winging among the white geese
in their practical formation, migrating to be here,
to keep house for you by the river …
i'll be home in time for the bees in their slow heavy
search for nectar, when the grass unfurls, nib tipped ~
you'll sense me as soft and fresh as a rose,
as gentle as a breeze of butterfly wings . . .
i'll return to honor daisies in the depths of innocence,
i'll be the raindrops rising dew-like on your brow ~
you'll see me sliding happily down a comely jacaranda,
as feral as the wind circling the crape myrtle, you'll
find me waiting, a small gray dove in the dovecot,
loving you, one lifetime after another.

Jamie Dedes of the United States is a former feature writer, columnist, and associate editor of a regional employment publication, and currently runs The Poet by Day, an information hub for poets and writers. She is the managing editor of The BeZine, published by The Bardo Group, a virtual arts collective that she founded. Jamie Dedes was featured in a lengthy interview on the Creative Nexus Radio Show where she was dubbed "Poetry Champion."

Poems by Francis Otole

Biceps and triceps

Broad chest and shoulders,
Toned thighs, forearms and skin.
Fifty kilograms of racism,
Fifty kilograms of brutality,
Fifty kilograms of poverty,
Fifty kilograms of imprisonment…
I lift them everyday…
I'm living my African dream.

Francis Otole is a Nigerian poet from the middle belt region of Benue state. He is an avid reader and lover of books. A graduate from the prestigious Benue State University, he is an educator, a researcher, an academician, a philanthropist, a Chaucerian scholar, and a pro-earth lover of nature and humanity.

Poems by Rokiah Hashim

I Am Sorry, Mir Rahman

That day
I had misunderstanding
With Mir Rahman from Srinagar
Because he refused
To give his real identity
And I was scared
To publish interview with him
In case I will be accused

aving links with Kashmiri militant Though many times
was duped
Because militant on one side
Are also freedom fighters on the other
Ah! Kashmir was once Paradise on earth But Mir Rahman said
Kashmir is now like paradise
During winter
With its frozen lake
And syikara* that couldn't be rowed
To ferry tourists
Like postcard photos of 70s
Not only that
Said Mir Rahman
His Fb accounts was ordered to be closed Every other month
Opened then closed
Opened again then closed again Opened and closed again
Closed and closed for good at last
Mir Rahman

Mounted on his postings
Photos of youngsters on street protests Or armies shooting at point blank
At the eyes of the young protesters
Or horrifying stories
Children and Muslim women
Raped by soldiers
Or stories of prominent University scholar Died of torture in prisons
Etc…etc….etc…..
Kashmir was a paradise
In 70s postcards
And now remained
Are painful stories
And miseries
And pain
And miseries
Said Mir Rahman

Mir, I am sorry
I didn't really understand
About your paradise
Which lost its beautiful glory
Long ago
And your miserable stories
Was buried for so long
By the bleeding of Palestine, Syria, Iraq, Afghanistan, Bosnia Herzegovinia, Kosovo. Etc….etc …etc….

*syikara are boats used to carry tourists in the lakes in Kashmir.

Rokiah Hashim from Malaysia writes using the name of Siti Ruqaiyah Hashim. Since 1987 her poems and short stories have been published by mainstream literature magazines and newspapers. She is also prolific in film and theatre criticism and since 2007 has written a column in a major national daily in Malaysia.

Poems by Mourad Faska

What Is Life?

The mysteries of life
Lie in its thrift,
Or rather in its rift.
Life is fear, anger,
Joy, exultation, and being tender.
One might exist but not LIVE!
everything is life but not everything,
a prodigal son might say: 'life is drinking to excess;
life is extravagance, flirtation, dalliance.'
A father might see it as dogma, prudence, stoicism.
A tender mother, but not so much wise,
May call it a 'bliss' from god,
Who defies it defies God himself!
Life is examination in the eyes of a priest,
And a path to heaven to an Imam.
Life in short is life itself!
Live, and live, and coexist,
With heart open and mind clear,
Lawn mow not,
And nature embrace !
That's the secret of life.

I Am a Wretched in the Earth of Riches

I am a wretched in the earth of riches,
 Our riches are now the rich's riches.
What am I! Hah
A man or a woman,
 I do not know anymore;
I, like Tirisias, a man for a moment
And a woman at another moment.
Perhaps I am a man more sinned against than sinning,
But I am what I am,
Greatness I never assumed,
A human being like you,
Flesh and bones,
With limbs, guts, and a face,
And in the same place we shall all embrace.
Why the world's riches go the rich,
And we poor fellows end up in a ditch.
Why these ignorant apes with their frightening looks,
With hooked noses and dark teeth,
 Think the world stands at their feet;
Their fine speeches are a blow
Far more worse than the whip,
Believe it or not,
Either on land or on the ship,
It is worse, worse than the whip.
They will smile, and smile,
And still be villains.

Flutter and Fly Away

The plain mornings
For the masses
May hold more beauty for a commoner,
What we usually see as regular
Turns into something of a peculiar
Interest to a lover of nature
 and wilderness.
Be like an eagle that hovers,
With wings wide open like a sail,
Aimlessly till
It spots a prey from afar;
For the moment you are
Conscious of your surroundings,
The joy fades away and dark
Starts to lurk from behind.
Love nature in itself
And nothing in excess,
Don't care a straw,
Run and look around,
Use your senses
      And sense the insensible,
Forget the past and
Enjoy the moment,
Break free from whatever is holding you back,
Flutter and fly away,
Aimlessly,
Aimlessly,
Until you find the way or it finds you!

Human beasts

In the wilderness,
Beasts feast upon other beasts,
With no regret or regard.
Hunger plays its part
And the weakest gets eaten by the fittest;
So are humans nowadays:
Those who have money
Have everything,
And those who have but a penny
Have nothing.
It's the same after all,
We're but animals in disguise,
Thinking civilization is the key,
While civilization is but a malady,
Nature is receding,
Birds are retreating,
And humans are increasing.
What to do,
Or where to start
Remains vague;
What a silent plague,
To have the illusion of living
Where your life is but a living
Inferno.

Mourad Faska of Morocco is a researcher with a BA in English Studies, currently doing a master's in English literature. He is a poet whose interests range across gothic literature, magic realism, science fiction and fantasy, ancient mythology, and peace-seeking literature, to name a few.

Poems by Smeetha Bhoumik

Making Fists and Opening Them Skyward

Purple & fuschia skies making
inner spaces a storm, fists
closing tightly and
then turning right around, opening
flower-like, a promise in them -
of fair liberating norms : hark skyward!

Clench, unclench, clench, a skyward
leap my eyes make, making
new interpretations of them,
in quaint settings where fists
are all we stake. Closing, opening
closing, a sudden spirited swirl and

fists have opened like flowers and
taken the skies by storm! Skyward
we move then, blooming, opening
hearts, breaking walls, and making
the world a beautiful place, fists,
yes, fists can do it all! Of them

There's no dearth, plenty of them
on this earth, to clench, unclench and
check the might that's ours. Fists
can tell if you're alive & looking skyward,

or feeling down in the dumps! Making
life a little easier, then opening

ways of seeing anew, fists opening
& closing can do a lot for you. In them
lie the power of coiled dreams, making
worlds out of thin air, and
the odds are you'll look skyward
in times of despair. Clench your fist,

and like Aladdin's genie, a way
will appear coiled tight & true, opening
when you see the light, a skyward
true blue. Maybe then you'll thank them
those critical of you, and
tread happy hues, joyous in your own making!

On dark days, leaping on light ,
making fists, and opening them skyward
Like flowers in the sky...

Smeetha Bhoumik of India is a poet, artist, editor, and publisher. She is the Founder of Women Empowered-India (WE) and Chief Editor of *EquiVerse Space – A Sound Home in Words*, the inaugural creative writing anthology from WE.

Poems by Melissa Begley

Joyful Night

Moon drops, snowdrops, raindrops tenderly eavesdrop on my teardrops. Broken heart and my teardrops will not thwart your departing since fate establishes a timeframe of your natural life.

Healthcare and prayers powerless to alleviate your destiny; therefore, my teardrops stream in the dark.

You are beyond holding me during the night and protecting me from all the fright. Smooches, embraces, and the delight of passion is a passing memory. My teardrops tumble down every day.

Where have you gone my robust and handsome man? It was not lust that kept us in sync, but the unique coherence of our connection. The disconnect has arrived and my teardrops stream during the night.

Inhale and exhale one more time for the reason the rhythm of your breath is almost gone. Eavesdrop on my heart and the beats are in cadence with my teardrops

Melissa Begley of the United States says she was humbled when Mbizo Chirasha expressed interest. Her background is in the healthcare industry.

Poems by Nsah Mala

Prophecies from Reptiles

Hails ourselves black botanists
We wine and dine with animals
We talk and listen to them
They talk and listen to us
We exchange wisdom with them
Listen comrades, reptiles say
Our kinsman has begun the chameleon game
His colours have begun changing
His thirsty tongue darting in and out
He fears armoured kingmakers
Will dethrone him if colours turn red.
Listen human brethren, reptiles say
Our kinsman has begun the snake dance
His venomous fangs are starving
He has uprooted family soldier ants
And crowned them family messengers
To sever them from village arsenals
Across the void of homing futures
We can hear galloping cloves of horses
We can hear clanging sounds of swords
We can hear wailing infants in Harare
Trapped in new battles against misery
And stagnation and oppression and torture
Trapped in endless clashes against overstays
Be warned human friends, reptiles say
From the bottom of the Zambesi

Nsah Mala is an award-winning writer, poet, motivational speaker, and youth leader from Cameroon. He is the author of three poetry collections, *Chaining Freedom* (2012), *Bites of Insanity* (2015), and *If You Must Fall Bush* (2016). His short story "Christmas Disappointment" won a prize from the Cameroonian Ministry of Arts and Culture in 2016.

Poems by Gorata Mighty Ntshwabi

A Dark Cloud Hovers Over Sudan

Volcanoes have erupted
Hurricanes have swapped away big dreams of the Sudanese
Rivers flood endless tears
Blood sheds painted their beautiful Sudan red
Young souls transformed into brutal monsters who massacre without pity
Women and girls heartlessly made to easily lose their God given treasures
All hearts bled in sorrow
African Ancestors left mother earth
Looking back
Looking back for freedom, peace and stability
Long live Sudan!

In a land filled with natural blessings
Berries, roots and treasures blossomed the atmosphere
All landed on the hands of selfish scavengers
Like selfish hyenas scrambled and never thought of tomorrow
In a land echoing gigantic voices of dictators
Diamond cartels and gold diggers
who never cared when hundreds and thousands
died and suffered from famine
Streets penetrated with gunfire, panic, whips and chaos
War devils who led with spears and arrows
Dictators with dark coated hearts
who smeared their horrific faces with tons and tons of oil and yet still remained shrunk

Long live Sudan!
Lord exalt my horn as I speak freedom
Distract my enemies as I speak nothing but truth
Today I instruct you all to stop pointing fingers at the white coats
As you must know you have brought poverty to your own people
Sudan has been transformed into racks by your own sharp dusty hands
And you go on enjoying bread and butter with your families when magnitudes of your
own blood continue to sleep with roaring empty stomachs
Your illiterate minds over controlled you shamefully
Where are the diamonds that once sparkled Sudanese motherland if one may ask?
The minerals that fertilized your mother land?
Long live Sudan!

Gorata Mighty Ntshwabi is a Botswana citizen, and author of an English poetry book *Exploring the Roots Poetry my Heritage Living Arts*. She holds a BA in social sciences with majors in sociology and psychology from Central University of Technology Free State in South Africa and a Post Graduate Diploma in Education in African Languages and Literature from the University of Botswana.She works for the Botswana Government as a Senior Gender Officer.

Poems by Ambily Omanakuttan

My Syria

Behold my kids
With no childhood.
Listen to their screams
Lost in the music of the bombs.
See their festering wounds
Like a paddy field with
scorched fissures.
Listen to the tales
Of fragmented bodies.
Look at the sky turning red
When village are bon fires.
See the ghost houses etched
On the carpets of blood
spread on the ground.
That is my Syria.

Ambily Omanakuttan is a protest poet, writer and activist from Kerala, India. She publishes articles in newspapers and magazines. Her poetry is published in magazines. She is an advocate of gender rights, human rights, and environmental conservation. She uses her poetry and essays to speak out and to amplify vulnerable communities. She is a literary revolutionary armed with her pen and poetry to free her people.

Poems by Michael Mwangi Macharia

It's Midnight in Yaounde

When the world wakes
From eternal unbroken reverie
To reality of a country
Torn apart by foreign tongues;
When the mass graves
Tucked with innocent villagers
Those that couldn't ballot
Celebrated with hail of bullets;
When the grim reality
Of hapless shepherds in collars
Armed with crucifixes and oil
Swept by the raging storm;
When a continent is roused
From slumber of inaction
Too shamed to look at itself
At the mirror another time;
Will there be a country left
To rebuild from dust and ashes?

The Common Man

Walking down the street ,
He Mouths common epithets
About 'us 'and' them'
Smiling with mindless glee
At the reckless ignominy
Flames of passion dancing
On grass thatched huts ;
Does he share in the victory
Or in the collective loss
Of shame and pride

City Rain

It's raining
On dark tarmac, concrete corridors
Multicolored umbrellas poke eyes
Crowds mile outside the big mall
That has everything for them all
The heavens are genial
Pouring sunshine and showers
To humans
of every rank and persuasion
In a world where there is enough
To meet everyone's need
But scarcely enough to whet greed.

Nightwarriors

They are night warriors
Who rise up at the wee hours
Nudged by stream of dreams
To freeze and capture vision
In words like seers of yore.
They are night warriors
Who tap on the soft key
Gazing at the white screen
Painting it with black letters
They are night warriors
Who listen to the silences
The music of the cricket
The dissonant croc from ponds
The harmony of mothernature
They are night warriors
Who seep knowledge of sages
That once cheered the alleys
Of the ancient cities
Pursued by lovers of knowledge
That was recorded in scrolls
The present seek to unravel.
They are night warriors
Who wake up to wonder
Sentries at the guardpost
Staring at magic
of starry evanescent skies...
They are night warriors
Who savour the fresh aroma
Of dewyspeckled rose at dawn

Listen to early morning sounds
Deliver the day's song
Before retreating to worldly realms.

Michael Mwangi Macharia is a prolific poet who was born and raised in the Nakuru county of the expansive Rift Valley in Kenya. He is a graduate of Moi University. He was anthologized in *Echoes Across the Valley* and has published in online journals. He also contributes articles to *Saturday Nation*.

Poems by Victor WeSonga

Recluse Poise

Oh politics, a tree with long stretched limbs
That struts to support prickly poisoned thorny twigs,
Holding blooming leaves and budding flowers, but
Feared by tendrils' soft phloem and xylem, dart
With bark of stem, a shining lustre of a people
Raised above the intricate network of fibrous that
Sips ground's moist, soil's nutrients n economy's minerals
Through roots irrigated by oozing blood,
Tears filling can, tears of feeling and emotions,
Tears that fuel fires of blooming leaves
Whose blood adorns red squares and streets,
For the budding flowers, even old,
Thriving on rifles that coughs, voices to silence, face
Of lives dispatched to early eternal phase.
Oh, recluse poise of Africa, what Psalm palms you plight?
Span of land that nature gives as north walks to south,
With soil as vast as East runs to West, starved of blight,
But why the political recluse in Harare? Whose mouth
And soil, hides ideas of brave men, fast of the
Ilk of Mujuru, Muzenda and Morgan, all rich
With women that wanders wide world at ease
Touching with touches of life that munches mere peace,
And brave alike, with zeal that justice preach
In face of tar turned flesh, down razing nation
Amidst red glown head torches that escort steel fists of brutes,
Oh! old ladies, descendants of faithful Sarah,
Holding to hoist high the tag to Abigail's obedience

In protection of Africa's hue in lieu of turmoil,
That forms nourishments that be of
Foyers of tribe that sites Africa's beauty in essence
Of weaning bad governance with presence
Of humanity without overt fake wake that mess!
Sharp is thy anger, oh thy whose language is brute violence,
How doth such language prefer thou?
One picked by those sans reason, full of insolence,
Bereft of diplomacy, even clout,
sans ability and means to commune, but
rapture with mystic heads full of dark cloud,
That abuse bhang, to shake astrocytes, for atrocities
With abused khat still in swollen cheeks,
And heavy in eyes schist of somnolence,
To lower humanity and raise superfluities.
Tarry and see, nurture this enclave few pacifists,
Let life and peace blossoms like floras of Savanna,
And stroll across the winding roads,
Unclench to free your steel fist,
Droop your hands, ease ire, drop iron rods,
All are your neighbours, at heart kindness list,
Whiten to clear soft your blood infested
Reddened eyes,
Cool your adrenaline, later be invested,
To your boiling blood, jacket its tubes with ice
Condense it's vapour, convert it to wisdom
And with it savour to enjoy; the freedom
Of the flows of Victoria Falls
The life in the wild, striped in Zebras, in
Giraffes whose necks hold high
Heads,with mouth's atop Heavenly Inn,
Enjoy powerful puffs off lion's mouth,

Savour seldom recluse poise of natural kinds,
Of the chirping egrets, on Mt. Nyangani's south
In the swishing lilting coasting winds
In which leaves play kissing, in dances of specific
Lyrics of rare rhumba, rare psalms, genre of Afric
Dressed in most pacific, dwells of Shona or Ndebele,
Luba or Mongo, Tutsi or Hutu,
Luhya or Kikuyu, oh, psalms that sums up Ubuntu!

Victor WeSonga of Kenya is a literature enthusiast and author of an unpublished anthology, *Militaristic Stairway*.

Poems by Munia Khan

A Leaders Path

He used to be a teacher of mathematics and chemistry
who was always aware of devilry's mystery
When darkness prevailed over Tanzanian soil,
the vines of nation suffered blight to spoil
the fruits of hope which could have been sweeter
But the harvester called poverty made it even bitter
The branches of life became fragile by bending
He came to impose measures to curb government spending
Thus, a patriot he remains caring for each resident
He is John Magufuli, the country's fifth president
When from Cholera his countrymen were dying,
he was the one- resolved to save money from flying
away with the jubilance of the land's independence
Now humanity loves to depend on the dependence
of peoples' dream for future on a great leaders' path,
When Tanzania is blessed to attain a rebirth

Munia Khan of Bangladesh is the author of three poetry collections, *Beyond The Vernal Mind, To Evince The Blue,* and *Versified*. Her works have been translated into various languages: Japanese, Romanian, Urdu, Italian, Dutch, Croatian, Spanish, Portuguese, Russian, Albanian, Finnish, Greek, Indonesian, Turkish, Bengali, and Irish.

Poems by Kabedoopong Piddo Ddibe'st

The Black Sun

The feathered arrows
Of the the lonely sun
Eloping from behind
Great graves of Africa;
Through the baptism of fire,
And living its fiery dreams:
I see it rising like Red Sea,
And its mustard tree passing
The tests of all times;
The feathery swords of the Sun,
Sleeping behind the great hills,
The great great graves of ancestors —
Rising red, growing red yellow
And setting all red,
Its piercing fingers pass
Across the face of the sky,
And blood red sweats drop;
I am amazed to hear
The dust of smoke rising,
And I am amazed to see
The rumbling of Jifungs
Marching to the desert
Eaten Somalia
And the forest swallowed Congo,
Marching for gold and fame,
I am amazed to smell
The rotting corpses of the worlds

Kabedoopong Piddo Ddibe'st is a published Ugandan poet, artist, and literature and English language teacher, an Acoli by tribe from Kitgum, Northern Uganda.

Poems by Anjum Wasim Dar

Do Not Throw Pebbles

Rain drops beating against the window
first with short intervals,then a steady-
down pour, a storm is a deafening roar
voices drowned, subdued will be raised
again, will rise and soar for the needy

humanity, half naked, soaked in pain
enchained in spirit, starved in poverty
'Do not throw pebbles at any color, for it
is strong, true, permanent, natural –
bonded with water, glass will not shatter

do not think me as different, I may be
similar in thought action and love,I may
be braver, but I have a heart, I know how
to play fair, and care, and share, I stare
at the world with surprise, I am tender

I am a person but through other people'
I know how to be human through other
humans, desert dark at night is gold
in daylight, serpents slither in rocks too
unseen unknown, black is gold and gold

black and I am a person only through

other people'-I am like the moon, lit
only by the sun, I am dark too, bonded
with Earth, inseparable, I shine for others
'I am a person only through other people'
Do not throw pebbles…

Anjum Wasim Dar was born in Srinagar (Indian Occupied)Kashmir, a migrant Pakistani, and was educated at St Anne's Presentation Convent Rawalpindi. Dar has been writing poems, articles, and stories since 1980 and was awarded a Poet of Merit Bronze Medal 2000 USA.

Poems by Karina Krenn

We Have Risen So Many Times

We have risen so many times of faded auroras;
between the shadows and flaps of things
that kill the mornings of illusions.
The price of life auctioned
and the death that walks,
after the poor people.
The anxiety of my word is such (They put me in it, if necessary),
that escapes my hands.
Maybe it's my certain potion for the one who has nothing,
for the one who lives sheltered from the burden.
For such a tiny eternity,
I try to abolish all distance;
open the successive doors of silences,
raising my voice … confronting injustice …
I bring life,
I decentralize the tricks,
I give you the password to the promised land:
We poets know when the seed is fertile
and we wrote poetry, in the memory of the peoples"
"Nos hemos levantado tantas veces
de auroras desteñidas;
entre las sombras y solapas de las cosas,
que asesinan las mañanas de ilusiones.
El precio de la vida subastado
y la muerte que anda,
tras la gente pobre.
Es tal la ansiedad de mi palabra

(que me amortajen en ella,
si es preciso),
que se me escapa de las manos.
Tal vez sea mi pócima certera
para el que nada tiene,
para aquel que habita
al abrigo del agobio.
Por una eternidad tan pequeñita,
intento abolir toda distancia;
abrir las puertas sucesivas
de silencios,
alzando mi voz…
confrontando la injusticia…
Apalabro la vida,
descentro las argucias,
le doy el santo y seña
a la tierra prometida:
Los poetas sabemos
cuando es fértil la semilla
y escribimos poesía,
en la memoria de los pueblos."

Karina Krenn is an Argentine writer, poet, and author of a novel titled *Inmarcesible*. She is a teacher of initial and middle levels of the Province of Córdoba, Co-Founder of Urpilitay foundation for orphan children, and cultural promoter and activist for women and people with disabilities. Krenn is convinced that poetry is the "weapon of massive construction" of a world that is possible for all.

Poems by Stacy Bannerman

Empty Boots and Baby Shoes

I am so tired of standing at memorials for soldiers; tired of weeping for the victims of this war.
I am tired of watching parents plant crosses for their dead children.
Day
After day
After godforsaken day.
I am tired of placing flowers in empty boots and baby shoes; of the way my body shakes at the first readings of the names that were added to the casualty count this week.
What's wearing me out is bearing witness to this war.
This foreverness of death, and the unrelenting loss.
It drains my spirit to meet the widow's eyes; to watch the fathers falter, falling to their knees…
Christ, that makes me weak.
To stand at the lip of the mouth of a grave that will never get enough catching mothers tears, a nation driving by the dead, is exhausting to my soul.

Stacy Bannerman of the United States is the author of *Homefront 911: How Families of Veterans Are Wounded by Our Wars* and *When the War Came Home*. Bannerman spearheaded the passage of several bills in the U.S. Congress, including the National Military Family Leave Act. She broke the national silence about combat veteran domestic violence.

Poems by Nicole Peyrafitte

Adonis Blue

A neck under your knee
you press you press you press
you press for eight minutes & 46 seconds a neck under your knee
you press you crush
the skin the muscles the nerves the veins whose?
say his name
George Floyd say his name
George Floyd under your knee
gasping for air
calling "mama mama"
panting "they'll kill me. they'll kill me," & you did
you crushed him under your knee
"they'll kill me. they'll kill me," he knew it
he felt it under your knee
slowly asphyxiated under your knee
your hands in your pockets your shades on your head you crushed a man
under your knee
his mouth foams his blood turns blue George Perry Floyd blue blue blue
not police blue not royal blue police-dead blue
under your knee
you crushed a man Derek Chauvin Chauvin Chauvin Chauvin
your French name an eponym of chauvinism excessive nationalistic violent
fervor & bigotry Nicolas Chauvin was a legendary
& possibly apocryphal French soldier
but you Derek Chauvin are not a fictional character
eighteen complaints already documented in your official files you & so
many other chauvinist pigs

strutting that "thin blue line" your hands in your pockets full of thick blue lies
under your knee
his mouth foams white under your knee
his blood turns blue George Perry Floyd

blue blue blue abducted life police-dead blue

you crushed George Perry Floyd bigot Chauvin
but this case will not be closed genuflection substantiation transformation
George Perry Floyd George Perry Floyd instant pupa
rises from hate splits from scene
a colony of Adonis blue butterflies takes wing
pollinates the great reveal
seeks justice searches for peace there is no end to this poem

George Perry Floyd Adonis blue
plant a watchman in

Nicole Peyrafitte is a multidisciplinary artist born in the French Pyrénées. Recent presentations include the 11 Women of Spirit at Salon Zürcher, New York City, and the 2017 multi-tier exhibition & live performance Peyrafitte / Joris: Domopoetic Works at Simoncini Gallery, Luxembourg. Peyrafitte's action paintings have been performed in a range of international venues. For more info: nicolepeyrafitte.com.

Poems by Georgette Howington

Haibun for Rice and the Farmers; WWII, 1943, Pampanga Province, Philippines

Lola Leanora Arceo served hot white rice, chicken adobo with Maragoso melon; the fragrant broth infused with memories of laughter, parties and dancing. My Mother, her Father, with six brothers and sisters sat on grass mats around the makeshift table in the bomb shelter as everyone lifted their rice bowls to eat. "Here in Pampanga," Lola said, "is where the best cooks are from!" Eyes twinkled, as she scooped food to her mouth, though she knew the ration of rice was almost gone.

Fiestas with music and food
when harvest is plenty; and
Mother's breasts are fat with milk.

The women's hands plunge into
the womb of earth transplanting
seedlings, praying rice will grow.

In war they cannot tend the fields,
a Mother cries for hungry children,
while a new dawn continues to rise.

Georgette Howington is a Filipina-American poet, gardener, naturalist, and conservationist. As a activist, in California and the San Francisco Bay Area, for over 30 years she has specialized in the conservation of secondary-cavity nesters such as the Western Bluebird. Georgette is a County Coordinator and State Assistant Program Director for the California Bluebird Recovery Program. Her poetry has been published in journals such as Sleet, Iodine, Poetry Express Magazine, and Poeming Pigeon.

Poems by Cassandra Swan

The Scorching Stage
(They're All Blood Red)

They're all blood red, the Junta!
Their faces cut as diamonds,
Hybridized with uneven facets.
Their mouths talking the talk,

Their arms lank as laburnum trails,
Their minds and legs Pavlovian,
Walking the walk.
Their souls and spirits lost

In hard-hearted machinations and
Indiscriminate alliances.
No chances, no risks without effect.
The blood must be shed; they're all blood-red.

Their words subliminally delivered,
The blood must be shed; they're all blood-red.
How empires adore excuses
              For momentous, violent pageantry!

 Avid uniforms, deadly costumes
Bound for a scorching stage;
Mud on faces, far away, say:
Have a nice day, have a nice day!

As psychopathic egos fuse,
grasping the dead as bundles of matches.
Metal chinks, exploding flesh, colliding with meteors
The blood must be shed; they're all blood-red.

A full moon hangs over war-torn lands
Like a giant white porcelain plate
Shattered by bazookas,
The shards stabbed God in the eye:

They're all blood-red, the enemy!
The dust never settles over broken cities.
The screams of the damned echo beyond death.
Still, the blood must be shed; as they're all blood red.

Hitler & the Wayward Shrink
(Notes at the end of the poem)

With your Nazi-jaw, tin-mine voice
Coat and helmet of giant turtles,
You gave only a nefarious gaze.
Your deleterious psyche rejected
The white cells of courtesy;
They possessed no aim in your veins.
A lightning tyrant, inexorable,
With ferret-heavy upper lip,
You motivated the ants to seize
The air in your Aryan presence.
You packed your chosen enemies
In a Brobdingnagian, rolling carronade,
To your bald-headed killing zone;
Sealed by your twisted-spider symbol,
That ran to each end of your song.

You cleaned your prey up for supper;
In a stew of rotting, gas-simmered schnitzel
Which curdled and clung, as
Putrid mist to the barbed-wire.
You were no amateur psychopath,
As you orchestrated a slow-death,
Nutcracker suite.
Yards of raw cloth
Folded back into the earth,
Your victims inhaled your toxic paradigm;
Piled high as reams of paper,
You claimed their flimsy, nameless skin.
Your own gasless bunker was

A Zarathustra, karma chamber.
No one could steal the deadly-nightshade,
As it multiplied in your polluted fervour.

I, the wayward shrink, erotisch,
Cavorted as a dominatrix on schnapps;
Confronted, seduced and, as a black-widow
Arachnid, slaughtered Hitler
In my jenseits slumber.
His genes have poisoned aeons;
Permeated generations of populations;
One in ten skittles has no compunction.
His kindred spirits convene
On political shelves; dusted down,
As old books, re-read, recycled,
Again and again, the rotluhend men.

Slick psychopaths emulate their heroes;
They rise as generations of blood
Hosing-up from the same clay;
Legions, armies, psychic vampires,
Influential as Arabian oil,
They are slithering around the globe.
Like offspring born without limbs,
The killing machines are born
With the absence of a conscience.
Hearken to the prophet;
Hitler and his doppelgangers are breeding
As flies in the Giant's Causeway.
Beware! They operate with only their
Character traits as an identifiable uniform.
When they parade, they feed on extreme cataplexy,

Provoking genocide or suicide:
Satan's psychopaths often wear a suit and tie!
The world must know their enemy!

Notes/Campaign: This poem accompanies a new campaign I am promoting for all politicians and political leaders to make it mandatory to undergo psychological profiling before they stand for office. The psychological profiling should be made public before the next election. This is a UK campaign to start with. My aim is for this to be a global vision to put an end to senseless wars. The poem may be shocking; however, war is shocking, genocide is shocking, and it has to end and we have to take responsibility for who is voted into positions of power. The world has to change, attitudes have to change, WAR IS NOT THE ANSWER! PEACE IS! VOTE CAREFULLY!

Cassandra Swan of the UK is an internationally acclaimed, widely published, award-winning poet, author, artist, revolutionary, visionary, political activist, medium, clairvoyant, PhD student, and former highly successful hypnotherapist.

Poems by Faleeha Hassan

Before my friend got killed

The sky actually was blue
The streets were more spacious
Women were sitting on the thresholds of their houses in the afternoon
Telling amazing stories to each other
The cafes were full of men's laughter
My father smiles as he tells her:
Don't take Faleeha to the hair salon
Give your hair the color of the sun
And leave the glamour of night to my daughter's hair
She smiles back and says
Her name is not poetic
If it were me, I would change it
We all laugh
My mother was more compassionate
She would say
Eat from one plate so your emotions will not be lost
And like ants on a candy bar, we would gather together
Oh, my friend
After your death
The world wore a garment of dust
The war had swept away the thresholds of our homes
Women now wear worries
Permanent sadness
Cafes are bustling with the songs of false victory
Men's voices are hoarse from smoke
And from drinking scorching defeats
Oh, my friend

Your death spread the snow color on my hair
If you had stayed a little bit longer
You would have seen how my name was won
 But death betrayed you
As it did my mother
And my father as well
All their advice fell on stone ears
Our lives filled up with wars, poverty, and exile
When I shout
Oh father ,
Mother,
Brother,
 Sister,
There is no echo coming back
And regret bites my heart
Oh, my friend
Can you stop your specter from dancing in my memory
Give me ten minutes to sleep
The smoke from the plane that killed you
Suffocates my days

Dedicated to my friend Mason Hassan Kamuna which she was killed during the Iraq-Iran war in 1985.

My Dangerous Memory

Oh, great
Whenever I dream of birds
The cages fly above my head
And I will need all my lifetime to know which cage belongs to my dream
And then whenever I try to remember my childhood
A bomb falls from my memory and crashes into my reality

"What a lovely sunny morning,"
I told the girl
She was jogging in the forest
She smiled at me
and said,
"A soldier's helmet is falling from your memory again."
"Don't worry. I have so many of them," I told her
Everything will be good
I say to myself
And I keep jogging from exile to exile
As my friends keep running from the battlefield of one war to another
And returning as pictures with black frames.

Faleeha Hassan is a poet, teacher, editor, writer, and playwright from Iraq. She is Iraqian diasporian living in the USA. She is the first woman to write poetry for children in Iraq. She received master's degree in Arabic literature, and has published 24 books. Her poems have been translated into 15 languages. She was nominated for a Pulitzer Prize in 2018.

Poems by Jane SpokenWord

Calling 911

Calling 911
'cause you're not comfortable?
Understandable
'cause you're so uptight.
Your ignorance betrays your white.
Their blackness scares you. There is no understanding while everybody's ranting.
Until there is conversation it's a volatile situation.
Tiki's lit
monsters on the loose
donald's spewing shit
whitey's dustin' of his noose.
What are you waiting for?
Call in 911 Black cat on the corner
singing his doo wop tune
minding his own do what he do.
Hoodie's in disguise
just walk on by.
Walk on by.
Walk on by. Calling 911
'cause you're not comfortable?
Understandable
'cause you're so uptight.
Calling on we who see.
Fight the powers that be
before they burn down the house.
Before they bring us down

to drown
in their swamp.
Tic Toc
Tic Toc
Fuse is slowly churning.
Tic Toc
Tic Toc
Brother's house is burning.
Write on.
Peace, Jane
"Communicating directly with the nerve endings of her hands her poetry shocks and thrills"

Street poet Jane SpokenWord is from the United States. Her performances represent the spoken word as it is meant to be experienced, raw, uncensored and thought provoking. She has done solos, to slams, duo's, trios, and bands, including a big band performance at the Whitney Museum with avant-garde maestro Cecil Taylor.

Poems by Doug Rawlings

On War Memorials

Corporate America
be forewarned:
We are your karma
We are your Orion
rising in the night sky
We are the scorpion
in your jackboot

Corporate America
be forewarned:
We will not buy
your bloody parades anymore
We refuse your worthless praise
We spit on
your war memorials

Corporate America
be forewarned:
We will not feed you
our bodies
our minds
our children
anymore

Corporate America
be forewarned:
If we have our way

(and we will)
the real war memorials
will rise
from your ashes

Walking the Wall

Note: My time in Vietnam started in early July, 1969 -- Wall panel number W21-- and ended in early August, 1970 -- panel W7, line 29-- a walk of about 25 paces past the names of around 9800 dead. I call this "walking The Wall."

Got to tell you that you're making me nervous
Every time you thank me for my service
I know you're trying to be nice and kind
But you are really, truly fucking with my mind

Trust me, it's not that I really care what you think
You who have had too much of their kool aid to drink
Trust me, you don't know shit about what service really means
You just need to know that nothing really is as it seems

So take a walk with me down the Wall some late evening
Where we can all listen to the ghostly young soldiers keening
But don't waste your time thanking them for their service
They just might tell you the truth -- all your wars are worthless

Unexploded Ordnance: A Ballad

For Chuck Searcy and the thousands of Vietnamese who have labored off
and on since 1975, working to undo what we have done

So I was maybe all of twenty-one
when they whipped me
into some kind of soul-less shape
Yet another one of America's
weeping mothers' sons
sent forth into this world
to raze, pillage, and rape

And now it's coming on
to another Christmas Eve
And songs of joy and peace
fill up our little town
How I ask myself
could I possibly believe
I could do what I did
and not reap what I had sown

In that land far away
from what I call home
a grandfather leads
his granddaughter by the hand
Into a field where we did
what had to be done

They trip into a searing heat
brighter than a thousand suns

Doug Rawlings co-founded Veterans For Peace in 1985. He has taught in high schools and at the University of Maine for over thirty years. He was with the 7/15th artillery in Viet Nam from 1969 to 1970.

Poems by Biko Iruti

Teach Me How to Keep a Woman Happy

I come as far as Kalokol,
To meet you, my tribesmen,
To seek your mediation at Lokichar,
To tell you of Akipe,
Akipe the evil one.

The evil one Akipe,
Has ruined it again,
Has caused it one more time,
I come with remorse, my fathers,
This time it is not me,
It is the evil one I assure you.

Yesterday before darkness overshadowed light,
Before daylight faded to night,
She was not herself again,
She was by herself,
She had locked herself in the kitchen,
In the whirring sparks of fire,
Speaking to herself and chanting cuss.

She says she is tired,
That she wants to go back to her father,
She says that she no longer loves me,
That her heart is void and loveless,
She says I am an inferior,
That I am lazy and impotent,

And I cannot sire her a son.
She says that I am a coward,
That I cannot skin a goat,
Or join my kin in the battle,
She says that my dangling balls are my weakness,
And she says I am not a man enough.

She hurls at me insults,
Scold me like Alimu, my daughter,
She throws ashes at me,
Boil water in our pots,
And she keeps promising me
That my head is suitable for soup,

She says that I know not how to keep
a wife happy,
That I am dull and ugly,
Like an elephant's husks,
That my performance is wanting,
That I collapse fast,
Sleep like a log,
And snore heavily like a bull.

I have spoken to my religious specialists ngimurok,
From both ends—ngimonia and ngichoro,
To sacrifice a bull to our ancestors,
Our ancestors ngipean or ngikaram,
To appease them.

Ngimurok say that ngikaram are not,
happy with me,
That they want human blood,

They need my only daughter Alimu as a sacrifice,
Lest Akipe destroys me with madness.
Tribesmen, help me know the ways of ngitalio,
Ngitalio—Our tradition,
That Akuj be happy with me,
That Akuj – Our God,
Bless me with a good wife,
Bless me with good children,
Bless me with many livestock,
And give me peace of nature.

Black Butterfly

The other brother
My brothers' brother son of my mother
He is white like corn
My brother talks in a rigid, mechanical voice
'Hey, black pot!' He fuss
He says I am black like oil
Dark and impotent
Slow and inept
Reprimand me as having diminutive brain
Punch his bosom
'Black and white' he says
He's a collegiate and an erudite
An only black island on a white sea
Always belligerent stinging with his tongue
'Hey, clogged mind!'
His certain bitterness serpentine my bosom

Dweller of dark heart
My mother's son is an enigma
Now that he has scooped from a whiteman's plate
Curls his lips into a lonely grimace
'Hey, soot!' What's that name, Lokopolae?'
He's now John James Johnny
His African name he has dropped
My brother feels he's a highly placed man
An erudite!
His haversack is asphyxiated with fat books
Oceanic names
William Shakespeare, Albert Einstein, Plato, Socrates, Aristotle
My brother cannot read black books
Written with black blood
And by black hands
He says such books are inferior –
Primitive and barbaric
'Mention one big boy of literature!'
Ngugi Wa Thiong'o, Taban lo Liyong, Okot p' Bitek, Chinua Achebe,
Wole Soyinka, Ken Walibora, Francis Imbuga – just to mention
'Shut up, Those are plagiarists!'
'Thieves of our language'
My brother has a new language
He speaks in a Whiteman's language
'Hey you, sooty Africans, copycats!
He cannot talk without mentioning my blackness
'Hey pot, offspring of dinosaur?'
'Tell me about the origin of your blackness, soot!'
My brother is a black butterfly
Educated on white soils
But milked all his brains
Identity, culture, and traditions!

Down Hill

Red lights –
Ruddy splendors scintillate the ink of night
Boom! Boom!
Wails of women and children thunders
Mayhem and trepidations
Rush –
Downhill, in valleys, and on mountains
Red lights-
Serpentining the darkling
Tinctures of blood in night
Flying and soiling leaves
Downhill bag of bones
Helluva rottenness
Unarmed public against a regime
Of astute political animals
Myriad fold dead
Lifes lacerated and owndoms battered
Cold lips in cold
Young men –
Revolutionists , fighters for liberation, justice seekers, nationalists
Like cockerel butchered
Like ghee lifes melt on cold soil
Sipping through constant jags
Swallowed by the hungry earth
Red lights-
Heads roll
From mountain peak to down hill
Fountains of red liquid
Scavenged skulls

Ambiance lull
The fringes wreak havoc
Spears flying and biting
Guns regurgitate fire
Bullets find homage in a national's bosom
Restlessness
Women rush
Toddlers on their backs
Imps in hands
Luggage's on shoulders and heads
And lamentations from their mouths
Iron sheets moan
From blaze
Fear maneuver everywhence
Rape intensifies
Women and girls
A sinister throng in such hard times
Wails and cries
Maidens lose maidenheads
On desperate accounts
And havoc
And insecurities
Of political apathy.

Biko Iruti is a fast-rising Kenyan poet, playwright, and short-fiction writer based in Nairobi. He is a student of English and literature at Moi University, a current features editor of "The 3rd Eye," a publishing press club at the university. Biko authored "The Love Realms," a romantic drama. He writes part-time for the Saturday Nation, a newspaper in Kenya.

Poems by Amanda Chikomerero Ranganawa

I Am Happy When I Am Alone

I am happy when l am alone
I sing when lm alone
I sing songs and melodies that tease my womanhood
I smile and laugh at my own jokes
A vibrant, chuckle, soprano full of joy and freedom
I am happy when l am alone
I walk naked when lm alone
I tease and admire my own beautiful skin
I let my hands wander on my nakedness
I dance when I am alone
I swing my own hips and touch my own breasts
I kiss my own lips…oooh when Im alone
I celebrate my sexuality when lm alone
I feel the roundness of my moons
I feel the silkiness of my thighs
I feel the curves of my smooth body
I feel the firmness of my silky creamy breasts
I let my fingers feel the wetness of my honey pot
I open my body to a sea of passion
I let myself drown in self pleasure
I am happy when l am alone
I get inspiration when I am alone
I get answers when lm alone
I sit there…think and all l see is clarity
I see change

I see the good in me
I see the mistakes I made
I see what makes me angry
I see what makes me happy
I am happy when lm alone
I feel powerful when I am alone
I read and meditate and pray
I seek the face of my Lord and l kneel down for him
I thank my God
I ask for grace and favour when I am alone
I am happy when I am alone
When l finally meet him
He that wants to be a part of my joy
He that wants to add to my happiness
I will be enough
My smile will be enough to make him smile
My laughter will be enough to make him laugh
My love will be enough to King him
My body will be enough
My personality will be enough
Bacause l am happy when I am alone
Model : The Melanin Queen

Take Me To The Beach

Take me back to the beach
Where the sun kisses my brown pearl skin
Planting it's tiny kisses on the arch of my back and thighs
Where the sunny breeze teases my cheeks and lips
Slowly caressing my round bossom
Take me back to the beach
Where l am a goddess
Where my beautiful face stops hearts from breathing
Where my tiny waist sings the song of free cocktails and drinks
Free food and gifts
Where the boys are buying
Scrambling for my attention
Take me back to the beach
Where my walk reminds them of Naomi Campbell
Where whistles, applause, and greetings follow me as l pass by
Where at the corner of my eye l see them
Black, White, Asian young and old man
Salivating at my sexy, smooth bottom
My beautiful round curves making them mourn in their pants
Take me back to the beach
Where it is legal to be the only crime in a man's heart
Where his partner's anger can't affect me
Where waiters pass me little notes and business cards from under their trays
Where l turn down their invitations
And watch them cry tears of sexual frustration
Where l laugh and sink back into my African sun
Take me back to the beach
Where l am the Melanin Queen

The wavery sea bowing down on my feet
The warm sand brushing my feet
The wind flirting with my beauty
And the sun crowning me
Take me back to the beach
Where l am the desire of all men
A fantasy of dreams never to happen
Where l chose who to share myself with
Where they all stare with grave jealousy
Where they can't stay mad
My beauty is a rare, sparkling black diamond
So, they clap hands when l pass by
Because l am a Woman
A beautiful black woman
All copy rights reserved.
Model : The Melanin Queen

Amanda Chikomerero Ranganawa aka the African Pen Princess is a young, female writer from Zimbabwe. She has been writing since age 9 and writes poetry, films, articles, novels, stories, songs, and online content.

Poems by Catherine Magodo-Mutukwa

Empty (For Women Who Lost Children)

She said,
I keep staring at this emptiness
where my 'whole' used to be
but
there's a 'hole' now
remembering
the 'everything' that imposed
'nothing' on me…
nothing to hold and nothing to
behold
except for the memories…
from the day I laid my eyes on
him to the last day I laid him
to rest,
My silence buried him,
watching it all in muffled stillness,
I was too afraid of the words
I~I would say
the words that were burning hot
things inside of me,
the words that are still burning
without ending…
For now
allow me a moment of sadness
and grief

Its been a while but the weight
of his loss weighs heavily on me
It's nestled in the creases of my
hollow heart,
searching for healing in the hidden
parts within me…
Maybe one day I will accept…but
for now I don't want to forget.

For Women on the Verge

Woman,
I'm searching for the
words
to put into your mouth
so that
you can find your voice
you're so desperately seeking for,
am here,
to peel away the layers of made-up strength,
brittle to the touch,
to access the exhausted human within you
who can't seem to keep up with the charade
so you can be gentle with yourself
Did you tell them?
Did you tell them about the many wars you
had to overcome this morning,
for your feet to touch the ground…
the effort it took to inhale and then exhale
when you would rather not …
about the dousing of a fire that once burnt
fiercely with intense conviction
when the heart was young and unscathed with
experience
about the crumbling down of boldness that you
keep trying to gather and
yet it keeps escaping with the fumes of
suffocated anger
Remember,
your anger does not need an explanation or
permission when you become un-stitched…

Home

The doors of my mind, there're refusing
to open
to uncover the mystery that makes
one understand
this tragedy that has become life at
home,
My HOME is on fire, it is burning…
BURNING I tell you!
Allow me to air my frustration, while
I sit here at the edge of dashed hopes.
Deep in the valley of despondency
where my thoughts remain oppressed and
my opinions suppressed and
all these emotions unexpressed,
"Powerless" needs no translation
the words I carry deep inside there're too
heavy, too heavy for pen and paper,
I can only petition our maker in the
eloquence of my silence.
An attempt to make sense of these agonies
has left so much unsaid
though I feel like shattering, simmering in
anger, struggling to conceal this mental anguish,
I begin to understand the value of my voice
to calm this storm…

Catherine Magodo-Mutukwa hails from an African city down in the southern hemisphere, in Zimbabwe. She is a mother, a poet/writer, a counselor and an advocate for the girl-child and women. She's very passionate about giving a voice to all those who struggle with the tongue which refuses to give them a language of feelings and expression.

Poems by Mbizo Chirasha

Empty Dream

I see rains of hatred pounding the face of juba
Socialists and mongers breakfasting human delicacies
Political drunkards lolling feeble voters to night mares and empty dreams
New born democrats buried without traces of memory under the hot hard granite of politics
Souls drooping in misery
When will sunlight cast blessings to these cemeteries?
Green lives decomposing in concrete corridors of history
The feet of history dragged in this grief laden earth.

Ethiopia

See talking slums
silenced tongues
freedom silenced
hope killed
a bling of ghettos
collapsed humanity

Mothers weeping,
under the compression of religion
trees dripping tears
Ethiopia your festering open wounds
you are my anger!
children burn in smoldering canisters of hunger
time opened new wounds of memories of old scars
chained on rocks of ignorance
you need a compass of decency

My poetry is a catalyst fermenting your injustices
into beverages of justice
you are my sadness!

Your heartbeat bleached in political fermentation
rhythm galvanized in furnaces of cultural myth
laughter imbibed by the rude stomach of the gun
culture crushing under the weight of globalization

Demons Grazing I

Democracy does not heal the syphilis of apartheid It never healed the hepatitis of racism
It is the ritual of the governed to govern
though they remain governed
Democracy, a word of the corrupted learned Democracy, a fart of the bullet signature of ballot
sting of the scorpion
Blood boiling stomachs of Darfur
Darfur you smell Nagasaki
Blood frothing hard rocky buttocks of Congo
Congo you sting Baghdad
Hunger pornographing breasts in Somalia
ministers dangling bellies
Poetry scattered in slums and ghettos
Word stitched between bullet and ballot
Grammar punctuated between slogan and vulgar
Democracy an oxymoron of Abacha's machete and madiba' bible
Hyperbole of Guantanamo bay and Robin Island

Demons Grazing II

Democracy
Freedom unearthed from apartheid intestines
A legacy that carried sorrows since the days of yelping baboons
and yapping dogs
Monrovia blooming legumes of blood in superstitions
of blood harvesting
Crocodiles basking in the east of political comfort zones
Afghan with the heart burn for freedom
Baboons laughing other baboons in political forests
Politicians crushing poverty under their feet
Polishing streets with the glitz of robots and rainbow sweet talk.

Kongo

Your past is a mint of blood and tears
Daughters tearing their way to decay
Sons castrated by poverty and superguns,
Kongo
Dream battered and bruised
Your conscience poliorised by oppressive -dans
Highways clogged by hatred and vendetta
Gutters donating stench and typhoid
Kongo,
Let my poetry feed your withering dreams for guns,
Insulting the tired memories of voters.

About the Editors

Mbizo CHIRASHA

Mbizo CHIRASHA, UNESCO-RILA Affiliate Artist. Freedom of Speech Fellow to PEN- Zentrum Deutschland, Germany. Alumni of the International Human Rights Arts Festival in New-York, USA. Literary Arts Activism Diplomatie. Globally Certified Arts Mediums Curator and Influencer. Internationally Published Page and Spoken Word Poet. Writer in Residence. Arts for Human Rights Catalyst. Core Team Member of the Bezine Arts and Humanities Project. His illustrious poetry, hybrid writings, political commentary, short fiction, book reviews and Arts Features are published in more than 400 spaces notably the Monk Arts and Soul in Magazine in United Kingdom. Atunis Poetry.com in Belgium. Demer press poetry series in Netherlands. World Poetry Almanac in Mongolia. Poesia journal in Slovenia. Bezine Arts and Humanities Webzine in USA. The Poet a Day in Brooklyn, USA. Litnet Writers Journal in South Africa. African Crayons in Nigeria. Poetry Bulawayo in Zimbabwe. Pulp-pit USA. The FictionalCafe international Journal, Texas USA. Best New African Poetry series in Zimbabwe, Zimbolicious Poetry Collections in Zimbabwe. Co-edited Street Voices International Publications with Andreas Weiland in Germany. Co-Edited Silent Voices Anthology, a Tribute to Chinua Achebe. Co-Edited the Corpses of Unity, solidarity collection to victimized Cameroonians with Nsah Mala. Curated and Edited the Zimbabwe We Want Poetry, Inside Digraceland speaking poetic truth to the Mugabe regime and other bad regimes. He owns the Time of the Poet blog zine, MIOMBOPUBLISHING that published the #GlobalCallforPeaceProject titled the Second of EARTH is Peace. A LETTER to the PRESIDENT his experimental resistance poetry collection was released in August 2019 by Mwanaka and Media Publishing. Co- Authored Whispering Woes

of Ganges and Zambezi with Sweta Vikram in India. Good Morning President his first poetry collection was published in 2011 by Zimbabwean published based in United Kingdom, Diaspora Publishers.COVID 19 Satansdeadly fart is forthcoming. Chirasha is Founder and the Chief Editor of Brave Voices Poetry Journal, https://bravevoicespress.home.blog and WOMAWORDS LITERARY PRESS,
https://womawordsliterarypress.home.blog

MORE INFORMATION visit,
https://en.wikipedia.org/wiki/Mbizo_Chirash

David Swanson

David Swanson is an author, activist, journalist, and radio host. He is the director of World BEYOND War, a global nonviolent movement to end war and establish a just and sustainable peace. He is campaign coordinator for RootsAction.org.

His books on war and peace include *Leaving World War II Behind* (an argument against the use of WWII as reason for more wars), *War Is A Lie* (a catalog of the types of falsehoods regularly told about wars), *War Is Never Just* (a refutation of just war theory), and *When the World Outlawed War* (an account of the 1920s peace movement and the creation of the Kellogg Briand Pact), as well as (co-author) *A Global Security System: An Alternative to War* (a vision of a world of nonviolent institutions).

Swanson blogs at DavidSwanson.org and WarIsACrime.org. He hosts a weekly radio show called Talk Nation Radio. He speaks frequently on the topic of war and peace, and engages in all kinds of nonviolent activism. He recently drafted a resolution urging Congress to move money from the military to human and environmental needs, rather than the reverse. Versions of the resolution were passed by several cities and by the U.S. Conference of Mayors. He also recently organized, with a lot of help from the Backbone Campaign, a flotilla of 50 kayaks that held banners on the Potomac River in front of the Pentagon reading "No wars for oil / No oil for wars."

Swanson is a Nobel Peace Prize nominee and was awarded the 2018 Peace Prize by the U.S. Peace Memorial Foundation. He holds a Master's degree in philosophy from the University of Virginia and has long lived and worked in Charlottesville, Virginia.

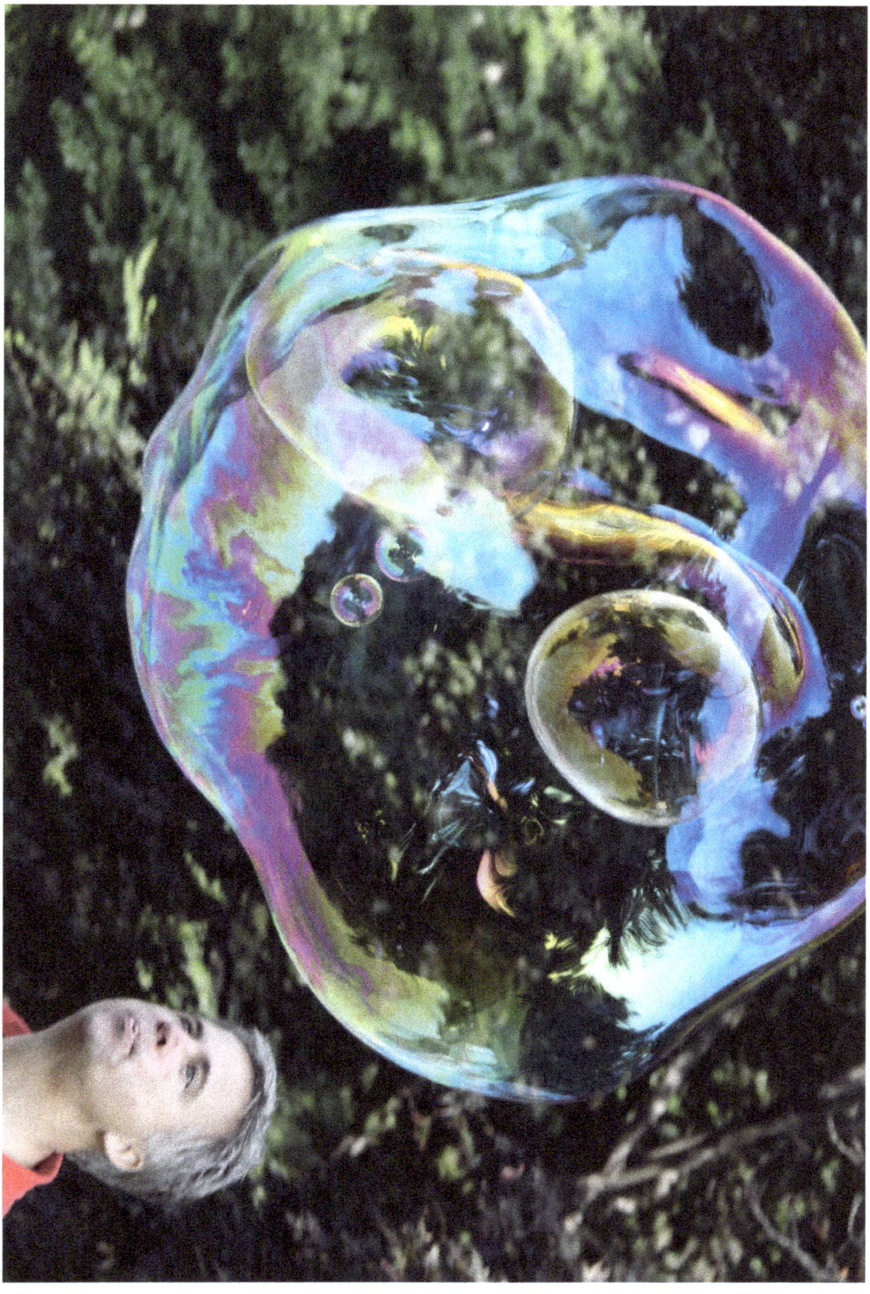

About *World BEYOND War*

Funds raised by this book will support the work of Mbizo Chirasha and of World BEYOND War.

World BEYOND War is a global nonviolent movement to end war and establish a just and sustainable peace. We aim to create awareness of popular support for ending war and to further develop that support. We work to advance the idea of not just preventing any particular war but abolishing the entire institution. We strive to replace a culture of war with one of peace in which nonviolent means of conflict resolution take the place of bloodshed.

World BEYOND War was begun January 1, 2014. We have chapters and affiliates around the world. While public opinion has moved against war, we intend to seize this moment to crystallize that opinion into a movement that spreads awareness that war can be ended, that its ending is hugely popular, that war should be ended as it endangers rather than protects — and harms rather than benefits — and that there are steps we can and must take to move toward war's reduction and abolition.

War is not ending on its own. It is being confronted by popular resistance. But too often that resistance takes the form of denouncing one war as unacceptable (in contrast to theoretical good wars), or opposing a war because it leaves a military ill-prepared for other wars, or rejecting a weapon or a tactic as less proper than others, or opposing wasteful military spending in favor of greater efficiency (as if the entire enterprise were not an economic waste and a moral abomination). Our goal is to support steps away from war and to spread understanding of them as just that — steps in the direction of war's elimination.

Peace is not free. We need your support if we are to reach all of those who would like to be with us or who can be persuaded to stand with us.

We are building something truly international, connecting people and organizations, and adding support to antiwar endeavors of all kinds around the world. This is a global campaign of education, lobbying, and nonviolent direct action.

Learn more about World BEYOND War at worldbeyondwar.org

CPSIA information can be obtained
at www.ICGtesting.com
Printed in the USA
BVHW011031131120
593255BV00005B/365